Memoir Of Jane Elizabeth Senior

Dorothea Murray Hughes

MEMOIR OF
JANE ELIZABETH SENIOR

BY

DOROTHEA M. HUGHES

BOSTON
PRESS OF GEO. H. ELLIS CO.
1916

DONNINGTON PRIORY, NEWBURY, BERKSHIRE.

PREFACE.

My mother has long cherished the hope that the life of her sister-in-law, Mrs. Nassau Senior, might some day be written and a younger generation given an idea of the noble woman whom she herself knew as a girl. She once asked my father to give her some recollections of his sister, and he jotted down the very brief sketch which is given later on; but during her married life my mother had too many cares ever to carry out the scheme. Now, however, she has had leisure to go over family letters and diaries with me, and we have picked out the most telling parts for this memoir.

We have found pitiably few things written by my aunt herself. Most of her friends and contemporaries are dead, and the letters they received from her have been destroyed. My grandmother Hughes, before she died, took the bundle containing her daughter's letters and burned them all on the hearthstone at Rugby, Tennessee. Therefore this memoir is fragmentary,— a letter here, a reference there, and whole decades skipped over with no record but a bare list of family deaths. It is a patchwork quilt, made out of pieces long tucked away in the garret, which by luck have escaped the mouse and the moth. Yet those who can see beauty in the fragments of old statues, may be glad to read what time has spared of the written records of Mrs. Senior's life.

DOROTHEA MURRAY HUGHES.

MILTON, MASSACHUSETTS, U.S.A.,
       January, 1916.

I have gratefully to acknowledge the kindness of Lady Ritchie for allowing me to use extracts from her sketches of Mrs. Senior.

I also wish to thank Mr. C. E. Maurice for permitting me to give portions of letters from Miss Octavia Hill.

D. M. H.

CONTENTS.

CONTENTS

LIST OF ILLUSTRATIONS.

MEMOIR OF JANE ELIZABETH SENIOR.

CHAPTER I.

EARLY LIFE.

Change is in the air in these days, and one wonders
if it has touched the Royal County of Berkshire.
There, in old times, white roads ran between green
meadows covered in May with buttercups. The pink
and white hawthorn formed hedges around the fields
where groups of oaks and elm trees cast long shadows
over the gold-sprinkled grass. Larks sang out of
sight in the blue sky, the wood pigeon called its soft
note in the spinneys, and blackbirds whistled loud and
clear. The land was watered by many streams which
had their rise at the foot of the chalk downs. They
were tranquil brooks inhabited by trout, and filled
with swaying water weeds which in June were covered
with tiny white blossoms.

In this peaceful countryside lay the parish of Uffington. In the early part of the nineteenth century the
vicar was the Rev. Thomas Hughes. Rather late in
life he had married Mary Ann Watts, whose clerical
ancestors had for generations been vicars of the same
parish. She had grown up caring for and lecturing
the people, much as her forefathers had done before

her. Dr. Hughes, a loving and most lovable man, had willingly given up a far larger parish and stipend to make her happy in her old home. He held at the same time, however, the position of Canon of St. Paul's Cathedral, and spent a portion of every year in London in the discharge of his duties. There, in their house at Amen corner, he and his wife held what might have been termed a London "salon," and received and entertained other canons, Sidney Smith and Barham, besides many celebrities, including the most beloved and most sought after man of their day, Sir Walter Scott. Mrs. Hughes, though tiny in stature, domineering of will, and economical of habits, had rare social gifts. She could charm her listeners with her legends and tales, and bring tears to their eyes with her songs.

John Hughes, the only son of this couple, was born in 1790. He grew up to be a typical English gentleman and scholar. He might have been trained to be an artist had he had his wish,—but in those days this was not considered the profession of a gentleman, and he was discouraged from turning his natural skill to account. He went through Oxford, and shortly after married a Miss Cook. She died within two years of their marriage, together with her baby daughter. He was so much broken by this double grief that his parents urged him to go abroad, and procured for him the tutorship of a scion of nobility, to whom he was to show the beauties of Italy and France. The scion proved so dull and intractable, so eager in pursuit of all that was better avoided, and so blind to all that was worth seeing, that he and his tutor soon parted company, the latter making his way homeward alone. This journey gave him the material for his book called "The Itinerary of Provence and the Rhone," which he illustrated with many sketches.

After some time he married Margaret Elizabeth Wilkinson, a generous, high-principled, quick-tempered, warm-hearted woman, whom her grandchildren still hold in loving remembrance.

Canon Hughes remodelled for his son an old farmhouse near his vicarage, and there were born four sons, George, Thomas, John, and Walter, and then on the tenth of December, 1828, the only daughter of the house, Jane Elizabeth.

The sun must have shone on her cradle at her birth, as the old saying goes, for throughout life she had the magic touch to turn sorrow into joy and bad fortune into good. Her happiness was unconquerable. If no fairy godmother endowed her,—fairies being even then out of date,—one may fancy a long line of ancestors passing by the cradle, and each leaving his or her best gift with the baby girl. From the old vicar, her grandfather, she inherited a lovely gentleness and sweetness of disposition; from her grandmother, the gift of song; from her father, his love of art, of modelling and drawing; and from her mother and her mother's people, sound health, a sturdy wholesome nature, practical capacity, and a warm, sympathetic heart.

In 1832 the good vicar died, and the whole circle at Uffington broke up. Old Madame Hughes lived in London for a time, and often revisited it later, when making her more permanent home at other places,— Wantage, then Kingston Lisle, and, finally, at Reading. John Hughes bought Donnington Priory near Newbury, and brought his wife and children there to a most happy home. At the time of the move, Jane already had one younger brother, William Hastings, and at Donnington were born two more, Henry and Arthur.

Among the seven brothers, two, Walter Scott and William Hastings, claimed her special affection. The former was the godson of the author. He was two years older than Jane to the day, and so like her that they were always thought of as twins. They had the same happy and sweet dispositions, the same brilliantly fair colouring, and the same love of music and singing. They were constantly together whenever he was at home during the school vacations. The other, Hastings, was her junior by five years, and very delicate when little. Her mothering instinct made her tend and care for him with the feeling that he belonged especially to her.

We give here a few words he wrote about her, nearly fifty years after, describing her at this time:—

. . . When I came to think what I could write of her early days, which should make clear to any one who did not know her, what she was to all of us, I was humiliated to find how little this was. . . .

John Hughes.

William Hastings Hughes.   Jane Elizabeth Hughes.

(From a water colour, taken in 1840, by Miss Meakin.)

One of the first memories which did come to me was of how, when she must have been about sixteen, and we three, eleven, nine and seven, she used to soften for us the wholesome, but despotic rule of the three Oxford boys (Walter, who was exactly two years older than herself, was milder and more like her, . . . he did not think it necessary to discipline us as the others did). But, on the other hand, she used often to have to shake her curls at us (all girls, I think, at that time in the country used to wear all round curls, whether they came naturally or had to be nursed in papers at night) for our misdemeanours, and never shirked giving us a good lecture when it was clearly needed. I think it must have been at this time, and mainly for this reason, that dear father called her "Miss Didactic," a title which stuck to her as long as she was a girl at home.

No picture of the family life at Donnington would be complete without showing something of the relations between the master and the mistress and their servants. Once a doctor, when called in to visit a sick child, declared the first thing he wanted to see was—not the child, but—the ice-chest! So a novelist, when painting a man's character, might well pass the parlour and dining-room by and draw his subject in the high-lights cast on him by the kitchen fire. Though we have no descriptions of scenes between Mr. John Hughes and his dependents, nor personal reminiscences by them, we have his own attitude towards them set down in plain English in the following extract from a letter to his wife:—

The rules of Christian conduct between master

and servant enjoin on the one hand the same civility
and propriety in giving our orders, and the same regard for the real comfort of servants and the good of
their bodies and souls, as for any other family friends
under our roofs; and on the other hand, the servant
is bound not only to diligence but strict obedience
and deference to the wishes of master and mistress,
behind their backs. When their duties are fulfilled,
the account is quit on both sides.

Of his wife's behaviour towards servants we have,
fortunately, a far fuller account. Thomas Hughes,
in describing Madame Brown in "Tom Brown's School
Days," painted his mother to the life. We insert the
vivid portrait here.

Madame Brown was a rare trainer of servants
and spent her time freely in the profession; for profession it was, and gave her more trouble by half than
many people take to earn a good income. Her servants were known and sought after for miles around.
Almost all the girls who attained a certain place in the
village school were taken by her, one or two at a time,
as house-maids, laundry-maids, nurse-maids or kitchen-
maids, and after a year or two of drilling were started
in life among the neighbouring families, with good
principles and good wardrobes.

One of the results of this system was the perpetual
despair of Mrs. Brown's own cook and maid, who no
sooner had a notable girl under her hands but "Missus"
was sure to find a good place for her and send her off,
taking in fresh importations from the school. Another
was that the house was always full of young girls with
clean, shining faces, who broke plates and scorched
linen, but made an atmosphere of cheerful homely
life about the place, good for every one who came

within its influence. Mrs. Brown loved young people, and in fact human creatures in general, above plate and linen. They were more like a lot of older children than servants and felt to her more as a mother or aunt than as a mistress.

Over and beyond this, Mrs. Hughes had no small hand in their early education. Soon after her move to Donnington she established a school there, and supported it largely from economies practised at the expense of herself and her own convenience. There the village children were taught their catechism and the three R's, besides the arts of sewing and mending. Good, plain morals also found their place in the curriculum.

Mrs. Hughes did not confine her care to the children of the parish, but lent a helping hand to all her poorer neighbours. Jane was soon old enough to accompany her mother to the homes of old or sick country folk. She absorbed almost unconsciously her mother's wisdom, and learned how to help poor people without taking away their independence, and how to encourage them in economical and thrifty ways. Mrs. Hughes' own housekeeping was, as we have seen, of a model kind. She had wholesome food—plenty of it, but no waste—and ran every department of the house with equal care for the comfort of the family and for the uninteresting details of economy. Even the robins and sparrows got their share of attention, and every day came to the bird-house for crumbs saved from the table. (It was one of the children's

great amusements to watch them as they fought over
the biggest bits; for be it understood that though
the English sparrow lords it over the other birds in
America, he meets his match in the English robin.)

Thus Jane, at home and abroad, had object lessons
which proved invaluable to her at every turn in her
after life, whether her way led through her own kitchen
or through the dormitories and dining-hall of a pauper
school.

Besides helping her mother Jane taught Sunday-
school. Mrs. Lloyd says in "Sunny Memories" that
Jane "called forth a quaint mixture of love and
respect" from her scholars "when herself almost a
child." This lady goes on, "Long will she be remembered in that neighbourhood, and by the many
friends so kindly welcomed by Mr. and Mrs. Hughes
at 'dear Donnington.'

"A sunny memory it is indeed to them all. The
old house and its charming garden, with a clear stream
winding through it! The archery ground and all its
happy associations—the hunt balls and last, not least,
the meeting of the Craven hounds at Donnington
Castle—a sight never to be forgotten!"

Mr. Hughes, as may be gathered from the foregoing, took a lively part in the sports of the neighbourhood: archery and hunting. His more serious business was that of county magistrate, and he regularly
attended the quarter sessions. This, however, only
occupied a small portion of his time, the rest being
entirely at his own disposal to spend in the usual

pursuits of a country gentleman,—in the care of his family and poorer neighbours, carving, sketching, reading, and the like. Once a year he superintended the dragging of the stream with home-made nets,—quite an undertaking, you may be sure!—for the purpose of clearing out the big fish that eat young trout. At times he must have found his freedom from any regular business routine a curse rather than a blessing; for, combined with natural indolence, he had an exacting conscience. His constant prayer, recurring again and again in his diaries, was, "May God deliver me from this demon of idleness." During his youth and middle age, however, he had none of that morbid consciousness of his own sin which darkened the last days of his life. His faith was sturdy and confident; his ideals of manliness were much the same as those we find in "Tom Brown's School Days"; and he met sorrow and adversity without flinching. He was wise with a practical wisdom born of his extreme honesty; for he feared to look no disagreeable facts in the face, and was free from that vanity which bids men lie to themselves. No man was ever born who more nearly lived up to the Hughes motto, "Y Gwir Yn Erbyn Y Byd," or "Truth against the World."

This memoir contains many of John Hughes' letters, which are valuable for the light they throw both on his own character and on his daughter's life. Unfortunately, we have none relating to Jane as a child. The following one to his wife brings us up to the period when Jane had been taken away from her

boarding school on account of ill health, and was
under her mother's care at Hastings, where the sea
air was effecting her cure.

MY DEAREST MARGARET:—

Yours just received. . . . At the present instant
it seems to me that the letting Jane go back to school
would be very wild, and I think Mayo would agree
with me. We may be thankful that she has escaped
as well as she has; and she may not be half as strong
as she fancies herself. If seriously ill again, we should
have exposed her to danger with our eyes open and all
for comparatively trifling considerations. . . . Surely
occasional masters would do all that could be wanted.
If not, may my hearty curse be on female accomplish-
ments. Life and health are of more consequence.
You know that I am anything but an alarmist, but,
in order to afford not to be so, I am vastly slow at
altering what for grave reasons seems a prudent line
of conduct. And I should at the present time (subject to skilful medical correction) favour the impression
that a young person so situated requires her mother's
vigilance for at least two years more, in order to grow
up strong—" 'Ware halloing till your fox has broken
cover." Talk to the boys about this—they have excellent sense, and love their sister like the apple of
their eyes; so, in God's name, it is quite as much
their affair as ours, tho' the sole responsibility, which
I do not shirk or shift, lies on my shoulders.

Thus Jane's *school* education was stopped in June,
1845, when she was not much over sixteen. In the
September of the same year, her education in the
school of society began. Her uncle, Thomas Wilkinson, took her abroad. She had thrown off her illness

by then, and a trip to Italy, it was thought, would completely re-establish her health. Thus she was sent on the Continent with only an old bachelor uncle to stand her in the stead of father, mother, and brothers— thrown on her own resources, adventurous yet homesick, gay yet lonely, to see for the first time the world beyond her ken. This journey forms the last chapter in her girlhood; for soon after her return she became engaged. Fortunately we have it written by her own hand. The following is her diary of the journey, and the words we read are those she would have spoken to her mother or best friend had either been present; but they were left far behind in England, and during the long months away from home she had only this diary for confidant.

Chapter II.

DIARY OF TRIP TO ITALY.

The journal begins:—

"Started from Usher's hotel, Suffolk St., on Monday 22d Sept., 1845, with Uncle Tom and David (a courier), leaving Mama, George, Tom, Uncle George and Aunt Wilkinson to lament our departure. At half past 10 we got into the train and a gentleman, seeing how staid and respectable a couple my Uncle Tom and myself were, begged us to take care of two little girls, who appeared instantly, one of them very pretty, the other a nice, merry little thing, but very frightened at the rail. Arrived at Southampton at half past one. We were to go in the 'Transport,' originally a Gibraltar vessel, and which looked remarkably uncomfortable, *i.e.* the cabins did. The captain was a very nice, jolly, fine-looking fellow. I secured a nasty berth, and we returned to an Hotel to dine—after which we went to see the carriage put on board—just in time to prevent its being scratched by being slung in.*

"At 7 I went below as I feared the night air. I lay down and knitted the fringe for 'rags' in the saloon. Uncle Tom went on board—felt 'woundy' cross, and wished myself comfortably back again; yes, with all dear Uncle Tom's kindness, I'd have given my ears not to have been going. The people began to arrive.

*As was then the custom, Thomas Wilkinson drove in his own carriage to the railway station, and had it conveyed by truck to Southampton and by packet to France. Horses and postilions were hired at each stage of the journey to Rome.

I went into the cabin and read: two gentlemen came
in to choose berths for two ladies, who came afterwards. The old gentleman was unhappy because
there was only one berth in the outer room; mine
being there I offered to give it up, for which he did
not thank me but said 'Oh'! I did give it up though
after all, though I got no thanks for so doing. The
people kept arriving; at half past nine the steward
was persuaded to begin preparing our tea, and just
as we were starting the welcome tea-pot arrived. The
people seemed very much surprised to see us eat, but
we did not mind them. I withdrew to my horrid
little hole—undressed and got in—but no sleep for
me. First an awful clatter overhead—then ladies
coming below; just as I began to doze, a lady like an
owl came below with her maid—they both lay down
on the sofa—the heat was intense, I was several times
on the point of fainting, but at length got to sleep.
Woke at about half past four, nearly suffocating.
Determined to lie there no longer—got up, dressed,
brushed, washed, did all but my dress. The lamp
went out with such a stench. Every one sick around
me, I felt faint and sick so begged the stewardess, who
was just as bad as the rest, to have the window opened
if she could, and then threw on my shawl and lay
down—went fast asleep thanks to washing and dressing, and the skylight being opened, and slept firmly
until eleven. Got up, had my dress done, packed my
bag, and went on deck, where I found Uncle Tom,
who had been there since three. We had a rough
passage, but it was calm enough then, a mizzling rain,
but Havre looked very well. On the pier were lots
of people watching us in. . . . I never saw so beastly
dirty a town. New smells at every turn, and each
more 'epouvantable' than the last. We . . . posted
off for the Hôtel de l'Europe. Washy soup with

vermicelli, fried sole, beef steaks spoiled with grease
and bad mushrooms, and some other queer made
dish, a delicious 'charlotte de pommes' and a capital
dessert formed our dinner. I thought I never should
get accustomed to the sour bread and washy soup,
but I now like both very well.

"*Wednesday, September 24.* After breakfast . . . we
. . . walked up the quays and looked at the shipping
and went into 'Notre Dame'. . . Several old women
were praying. It seems to me that none but old
women go to church in France. . . . We went to the
pier to get on board the Honfleur steamer. The carriage was already put on—we sat down and watched
the arrivals: a man and woman and two pretty French
servants. The man was refusing in a very squeaky
voice to give anything to a porter who had helped
bring his wife's innumerable packages from the hotel.
The woman took about half an hour arranging herself,
parcels, servant and lap-dog. Then a lot of old and
young women and men came clattering down the
ladder—then two fat dirty old men, who smoked and
spit immensely on board, and 3 or 4 boys—such
creatures; dressed like men, and the eldest could not
have been 17—a kind of down on the lips of the two
eldest denoted an intense amount of shaving, (of
hardly any avail), their coats tight in the waist,
trowsers strapped down so that they could not stoop,
kid gloves, canes, &c., amused me much. I have
been now a week in France—perhaps I am as yet no
judge, perhaps not an impartial one—but it seems to
me that the women are nearly all ugly and the men
small and ill made. The plan of the women wearing
nothing out of doors but caps, makes them as sun-
burnt as men, and they are therefore so ugly I suppose."
(It is amusing to speculate as to what she would have
said to the modern hatless young lady.)

At Honfleur Mr. Wilkinson and his niece had post horses harnessed to their private carriage and started for Caen. It was their plan to post all the way to Rome, visiting Tours, Bordeaux, Toulouse, Montpellier, Nice, Genoa, Pisa, Florence, and other points of interest on their way.

Of the journey to Caen, Jane writes:—

"The horses in general are wretched things. Uncle says they are very strong, but they are rough, unbrushed, ungentlemanly looking animals, generally grey, and covered with dirt, and the harness kept together with old bits of rope and an inch thick in mud. The third horse goes before the other two and they call him the 'pallonier.' The fastening in the horses at each stage takes a very long time, though there are generally five people doing it, and invariably before you have got 200 yards the postilion has to get off and do something to the harness of the 'pallonier.' As we got further south the post-boys wore very large clumsy boots—each weighing, as David told us, 15 lbs. At the end of this post the postilion wanting to see what Uncle Tom was made of, wanted more than his due; Uncle Tom called for the post master, a very bad, red-nosed looking fellow, who took the postilion's part. I sat dying with laughter in the corner of the carriage. Uncle Tom got angry, produced the post book and showed them the due. He ended by giving just what was in the book which was less than he had offered him at first. . . . At length we got off. The lamps are hung across the streets, as they are in John Potter's pictures of abroad, which I never could make out quite till now. It grew dark, the glass windows were shut, and I went to sleep till we arrived at Caen, a little before ten. . . ."

Of the road from Caen to Le Mans, she writes:—

"The country was very like Berkshire, and I often thought of home and our people, till I made myself quite melancholy, and as the rosy light faded away I could have cried, but instead of that I determined to go to sleep, which I did till we arrived at Le Mans, at half past eight."

The next day she visited the cathedral. When reading her reflections on it, we must remember her extreme youth.

"It was splendid—very lofty and roomy, gave one an idea of immense space, but what struck me most was the painted glass—the whole of the windows in the choir part of the church, were of stained glass. This threw a calm purple light over the splendid roof and columns, which gave one a feeling of awe almost. I could not have spoken aloud for anything. . . . How sad, that such a noble edifice should be only one of the many in which superstition, not God, is worshipped. How can people, with the usual degree of common reasoning sense, when they come to years of reflection, be Roman Catholics? They must see the impossibility of a human being absolving them from their sins, they must see that God is served by the heart, not by outward show, &c. Has the Almighty hardened their hearts, that they should not see and understand, believe and be saved?"

On Saturday, September 28, Jane and her uncle left Le Mans, and arrived that night at Tours. On Sunday they went to hear Mass, which she describes as follows:—

". . . Some part of the service was very splendid and impressive. The priests and choristers sing and then the organ answers them. There were two boys with really heavenly voices. I was becoming very much interested indeed in this beautiful part of the service, the incense was filling the church, and the alternate voices and organ were succeeding each other as the procession moved down the middle aisle of the church near where I was sitting. We all rose as they passed, the priests in splendid crimson velvet and gold dresses —the boys bearing immense tapers, and a golden crucifix borne by a priest in white;—but in a moment I was brought to earth again. An old priest, with a fine outline of face, though with a very unclerical expression, stopped chanting; and just down on the floor in God's house! he spit!! I never was more shocked. . . . I particularly looked at the countenance of each priest as he brushed by me, moving very slowly. They looked, all, every one of them, as if their best affections were dried up. . . . I thought too how like their clothing was to their religion. The most splendid crimson and gold, over such sadly dirty-looking bodies, their hair, hands, and faces were very dirty—and in their religion they hide the impurity of the inside of the cup and the platter, with fine processions and ceremonies which are imposing to a great extent."

It is amusing to note here a passage from her report on the education of pauper girls, which shows the woman of forty-five to have had the same heart as the girl of sixteen.

"The girls wore one shift day and night for a week. When ·the state of the girls' under-garments is contrasted with the often spotless purity of the pinafores in which they appear in the schoolroom . . . I cannot but think it is a sad example of cleaning the outside of the cup and platter only."

It rained all during the Sunday in Tours, and Jane confides to her diary that she feels England-sick and has the blues. She inserts the following in her account of the day:—

"I have just been reading back—how egotistical I have been—but no one shall read this but myself."

She remarks with high disapproval the European "disregard of Sunday,"—"buying and selling going on as usual. It was very unpleasant to English feelings." She goes on to describe some of her fellow travellers.

"Our party at the table d'hôte was an elderly young lady, . . . a horrid discontented old brute of a man, and three other young men, with moustaches. The old man, slightly assisted by the others, kept abusing 'Sophie,' the civil little maid, because he said the dinner was disgracefully bad—and eating like a pointer all the time. . . . He talked of women and abused a very pretty shop-woman because she would not talk to him, and squeeze his hand as she served him. . . . He set up for being knowing because he doubted honour either in woman or man, and talked of marriage in a ridiculous way—saying that a wife ought to be happy to hold her husband's handkerchief for him. A wife ought not to be a man's slave (although she ought to obey him implicitly), but his friend, companion, comforter, in short his wife. . . . I never saw people eat as these do. I thought I had a precious twist till I came here, but it seems that I eat nothing comparatively. This lady eat of every single thing. I was very happy to leave the table for I do not like that style of conversation, but I had to laugh over them with Uncle Tom who, however, had been as annoyed as myself."

On the way to Poitiers, the next day, she expresses her mind freely on the people she sees.

"The women had a dirty handkerchief round their heads, no shoes or stockings, dreadfully unclean legs (bare) and sabots. They hardly looked human, and they were generally driving pigs, the pigs being as unlike pigs, as the women were to women. . . . The postilions are the best sort of looking men. The immense amount of beard and moustache which some of the men wear is horrid. I cannot bear a man without any whisker, but a bare faced man is far preferable to these monkey looking things. . . . The oxen are very pretty animals, but the poor things are yoked together by the horns, and pull with their heads, it must hurt them—but that would not make any impression on a Frenchman. . . . A small mule pulls a load of wood—sometimes stone—which would be a good burden for three horses, I declare, and when they are accustomed to the whip and don't mind it, I have seen the postilions beat one place on their backs with the butt end of the whip till the animals must be fearfully bruised. It makes my blood boil. I could witness the torture of such men with heartfelt delight. I have longed to see the horses throw them and kill them—a shocking feeling for a woman to have—but I can't help it."

Her first sight of Bordeaux made a great impression on her.

"The sun was setting—purple, golden and crimson
lights were shining over the town—a haze hung over
the houses, and above it towered up splendid old
black-looking spires, and masses of fine architecture.
The river, which is very broad and clear, was filled
with shipping and the cliffs on our left were covered
with fine trees. I wish Scott had seen and described
Bordeaux as we saw it."

Unlike the average girl of to-day, she evidently
enjoyed the long descriptions of scenery in which
Scott indulges.

At Toulouse she went to the opera. She does not
appear to have had that painful shyness which one
would have expected in a country-bred English lass,
for she writes:—

"Next me sat an old gentleman smelling awfully of
garlic, but very civil. After the end of the first part
he began talking to me, and told me amongst other
things that the people of Toulouse were not so polite
as those of Bordeaux, but that they were better than
those of Marseilles, who were horrid. Of course I
bowed at him and said that I could not feel that the
Toulousians were less polite than the Bordeaux people
—he seemed to take the little compliment to himself
very well, and I congratulated myself on having made
it. He was very curious, and found out all we had
been doing and all we were going to do by skilful questions which made me laugh to myself greatly as I
answered them, for I did not see why the polite old
thing should not have his curiosity satisfied, as it did
me no harm; and of course I was delighted with him
for telling me I spoke French well."

They had arrived on October 9 at Toulouse, and spent all of the next day there. At table d'hôte she notes a

"young man began talking about and abusing France. . . . 'Woe be to the bird that fouls his own nest.' He abused people, hotels, &c., &c., freely, perhaps when he is older he will be wiser, poor fellow,—and if he loves England and English manners, &c., why does he not follow their example, wear a clean shirt, cut nails, wash hands, brush and cut hair, and shave his moustache off? Not but that he is right in liking the English better than any other nation, but France is his country and he ought to stand up for it."

Later she finds out that the young man is a Russian.

"He is therefore quite right," she remarks, "to like England and hate France. I like him now! how one's opinion changes. He is a capital linguist and very clever, and was cleaned up at dinner."

In recalling the conversation she had with him, she says:—

"Talking of meeting one's countrymen reminds me. The Russian was saying that the only one of his people he met in England when he was travelling there was a very dirty Jew, who spoke his language abominably, but still 'I was so glad to hear my language that I really did kiss him.' The very best proof he could have given of his patriotic kind of joy—for to kiss a very dirty Jew, must require some degree of courage, and the impulse of the moment must have been very strong."

After almost three weeks' experience of table d'hôte, she comments:—

"It is very different talking to a gentleman and a lady. If the gentleman wishes to be agreeable he must talk a great deal, and then it is very easy for the lady to answer, and do a certain portion of the agreeable—and if the man does not take trouble to converse properly, the lady need only answer him and hold her tongue.   But with two ladies it is quite different."

On Saturday, October 11, she writes:—

"The entrance to Montpellier was charming. . . . The white town on the hill, with a splendid aqueduct along the valley, high mountains on the left and blue sea on the right with the sun setting was more beautiful than anything I ever saw except Bordeaux as we entered it.
"*Sunday, October 12th.*   Got up at half past six to have a good time for ablutions, &c. . . . I could truly say with Papa,

'Why do them fleas torment me so!
I ne'er did they no harms,
They used to come by twos and threes
But now they come by swarms.'"

On Monday, October 13, they left Montpellier for Nismes.   She observes:—

"I never heard dogs make such a noise as the French ones.   Even as one drives along the road every cur comes yapping after the horses' heels, and this night I thought they never would have done yelling and barking.   I am sure the poor old setter whom I fed under the table, at the table d'hôte yesterday, could not be one of the noisy brutes I heard."

Having taken rooms at the Hôtel de l'Europe at Nismes,

"we sent for the blanchisseuse and gave her the things and then sallied out. We went through some stinking streets, and got up by the Papal Palace, now turned into a barrack and prison. . . .

"As we passed the barracks something happened which made me boil with rage. The Russian was right, the French are *brute beasts;* I hate them, and will hate them from this evening. I would forgive them spitting on the floor, and singing at the theatre, and never remember their dirty, greedy habits, but this has made me hate them. A lot of soldiers were standing and sitting round the door of the *papal* barracks—a dear, splendid, noble-looking dog came up and was entering quietly into the barracks when a devil incarnate (I could wish he might be one eternally, but will not) of a soldier ran at him and I *suppose* wounded him, for though the noble dog made no noise, yet the man came out shaking the blood off his bayonet, and his companions set off laughing. I never felt so disgusted, so fiercely irate, as at this."

On Wednesday, October 15, they drove over from Avignon to Vaucluse. Jane writes:—

"Vaucluse is a most singularly situated spot. . . . We wound in and out amongst rocks by the side of the most clear, sparkling, dashing stream ever beheld or conceived till we got partly through the village to the Hôtel de Petrache et Laure. Here we left our carriage and marched up the side of the stream to get to the fountain. . . . The rocks are high and wild, at their foot grow very nice trees and then the stream rushed along, sometimes over bits of rock, sometimes

as calm as a mill pool. The valley is a complete
'cul de sac,' and at the extreme end is the fountain.
It must be immensely deep, and looks so cold and
still as almost to make one uncomfortable to approach
it. . . . The fish in this most perfect river are worthy
of it. I wish 'the brothers' could come here and
fish, and bring me. I should like nothing better
than to revisit it. We sauntered back to our Inn and
ordered dinner, and then went a short way up the
town—never was seen such a beastly place—poor
Petrarch! you must have often been 'stunk out' and
have retreated to your beautiful fountain, as much
to escape the smells, as to think of Laura and write
poetry. . . ."

At Antibes, the last stage in France, she writes:—

"I was very glad of my supper, and got an English
cooked mutton chop and potatoes with the meat! a
luxury which I fully appreciated. After dinner they
gave us the 'confiture de menage' which Grandmama
mentioned to me—and very good it was. Uncle discovered how it was made—grapes boiled very long and
very slowly in treacle. I thought it capital and shall
get Mama to make it." [Perhaps some venturesome
person may like to try the receipt.]

She describes her journey of the following day:—

". . . A more lovely and enjoyable drive I never had.
It reminded me of the early morning at Salterton, and
going down to bathe with dear Fan* and old Matty."

Of the journey from Nice to Oneglia she writes:—

"It was a beautiful day, and the sea as calm as a
pond, the ripples not breaking on the shore even. One

* A schoolmate, Miss Anne Frances Ford, who afterwards
married her brother Tom.

part reminded me very much of the 'Signal post glen'
[at school] which Fan and I used to beg poor Miss
Beale to let us scramble up and down, only it was
not so beautiful as the old glen. I fancied Fan and
myself rushing about as we used, joined by hardly
any of the others—alas for their bad taste."

The following suggests a very pretty picture of a
scene at Oneglia, the startlingly fair girl surrounded by
the swarthy little Italian children—though evidently
the writer did not view it in a romantic light.

"Then we went down again by the pier—the children
so astonished at seeing English, that they appeared to
think we could not be real, and came touching my
shawl, poor little things, apparently expecting even
such a substantial bit of flesh as myself to melt away
at being touched, whereby I got sundry fleas."

At Genoa they met their friends the W.'s, who ac-
companied them to the post-office.

"The first letter I saw was one for me. I seized and
opened it,—Mama and Tom—he enclosed a little note
which I read directly. I nearly screamed with joy.
Fan is coming at Xmas—the old man came round
splendidly; they are to meet and I suppose to write,
but Tom was so mad that his scrap says nothing
hardly, but enough to send me mad with joy. We set
off walking, and I answered Mr. W—— very queerly
in my strange happiness. . . . This is indeed a bright
day, hearing of this and getting so beautiful a present."

The present was a "most beautiful bracelet of light
coral" from "kind dear Uncle." She also took great
satisfaction in the gifts she had bought for friends at

home. She spent twenty-two francs on coral—"an
immense sum" for her, but to her delight she found she
had made a bargain. "Captain Kearns said that he
had given four and a half francs for a little hand without the dagger," while she "only gave sixteen and a
half for 10 little devices."

At Genoa Mr. Wilkinson parted company with
David, the courier, who had become too lazy. Giovanni was his successor.

At Chiavari she writes:—

"I caught about 8 mosquitoes going to bed, and
letting down my mosquito curtains felt sure of being
safe. A brute of a cat made more unearthly howling
than ever was heard before, but I soon got to sleep. . . .
Alas for the fancied security of mortals. I went to
bed under my mosquito curtains in the full security
of not being bitten, I woke at four bitten to death
and awakened by their triumphant buzzing, for they
had got under the curtains."

From Chiavari they went to Sarzana, and from
Sarzana to Carrara, where they walked over to see the
marble quarries.

"Our guide was astonished at my being so 'svelta'
and not wanting his arm and expected me to do like
other ladies who came here, to sit down every five
minutes. He cannot be accustomed to English
women! The marble rocks are very singular, in wild
ridges, without the least verdure. The marble, the
purest, most beautiful transparent white."

Of the journey between Carrara and Lucca she
writes:—

"About every ten miles this day we got into new territory. It was nothing for poor Uncle but unlocking the desk and giving out the pass-port, and giving a franc to the douanier for believing Uncle Tom's word, that we had nothing contraband. The custom-house people were very civil though and did not look at a thing, so great an effect has a single franc.

"*Thursday, October 30th.* Lucca. Slept beautifully. Breakfast in our odd little salon, and a very good one too, we got toast for a wonder and the best butter we have had for a long time. My journal is a very gormandising one, mentioning all the eating, but n'importe, what comes into my head must go down, or it won't be natural. Uncle's cold better. . . . Uncle went to the banker's and I sewed up holes in my gloves, and ran strings of pack thread into my black silk bag. The stocking mending is the fun! I never could have patience to darn, and now I have not time. I have learnt to button my petticoat! oh! wonderful, and can lace my gown half way up, and hook and eye it all the way. After Uncle's return we started for Pisa. . . . I wonder more and more every day at the hardiness of the women, we saw several (as we have indeed all the way along) standing in cold water with naked legs and feet, draggled petticoats, with a hot sun on their heads, banging the dirty clothes in the water (intending this for washing). I wonder they do not die under such work. . . .

"*Friday, October 31st.* Uncle quite better. Mended more gloves; it is like the bloody key in Bluebeard— as fast as I mend one side the other is in holes, as fast as Fatima cleaned one side the other got bloody. . . . Then we went to the Campo Santo, a most beautiful, very interesting old building built about 1200. . . . The walls of the arcades are covered with frescos. . . . I must mention two frescos which struck me as very ludicrous. . . . One of them is 'The Triumph of Death.' In the air above the earth (where people are going on as usual) devils and angels are quarrelling and fighting for the bodies of dead people. An Angel and a devil are playing 'French and English,' the body of a fat old friar being the cord. The poor old thing looks as if he would prefer going straight to Hell than to be tugged about so with only a chance of getting to Heaven. Then there are diminutive angels carrying in their arms large fat men and women, and one devil is so loaded that he has got a man upside down and is conveying him to Hell by his heel. The other disgusting old fresco is 'The Last Judgment.' . . . Solomon, who has got his head and shoulders out of a trap door, does not in the least know if he is to go to Heaven or Hell. Then there is one bad man who has got among the good people, and an angel had seized him by the hair and is showing him the way to the Infernal regions. Hell is represented as brim full chiefly of women, and serpents green and yellow are twining among them and biting them in unheard of ways. One woman is having her head held back by the hair by one devil, while another is pulling out her teeth with immense pincers. . . ."

They arrived at Florence November 3. Jane writes enthusiastically about the paintings:—

"Uncle says he does not think I like pictures much. How very much mistaken he is for once! I do not talk much of them, for I am afraid of committing myself, my taste not being as formed as his, but some pictures I enjoy too well to express my pleasure."

On November 5 they visited the Palazzo Pitti, where Jane says, "To mention all that struck me would fill books, so I must stick to a few." Then follows a long list of pictures with exclamation marks after each one. She had explained earlier in her diary that raptures grew tiresome, and therefore she had chosen this convenient form of abbreviation.

They stayed in Florence ten days. On November 6 Jane writes:—

"At dinner Mr. and Mrs. W—— appeared to my joy, and I at last recognised in a mad Tom-cat looking moustached thing, Mr. S. P.! of Oxford notoriety. Poor old W—— very miserable, almost crying at having got an uncomfortable garret upstairs. The German lady next him eat to-day with her knife. The Countess Guacciolo at table, she is very handsome, but not a finished lady. I finished my letter to Mama telling her of my seeing Mr. Tom-cat P. . . .

"At the bottom of the table sat a young fellow exactly like the pictures of Prince Albert; opposite those wretches who have always been there, spitting and making themselves very disagreeable by such beastlinesses. Between me and Mrs. W—— sat an Englishman, who I hear is in the Indian army, a charming man I thought; perhaps he talked a little too much, but he was very gentlemanly, and I was delighted with him. He has been to Egypt, Jerusalem, &c., and is going to Rome, Portugal and Spain as fast as possible and then home to his 'dear England.' Dear man, he loves his country as I do; I could have kissed him, so pleased was I to meet one who sympathised with me. He has been almost everywhere, and he has found nothing so comfortable as England, nothing so agreeable, nothing more beautiful, and nothing so lovely as his country-women. . . . Talking of the opera he said that [when abroad] many English people, even ladies, go on Sunday night, and added that he would never do so, Sunday was Sunday. . . . He is a capital fellow—for an officer and a man who has been so much abroad to feel and act thus is really delightful. I hope he will sit next me to-morrow, I like him so very much.

"*Sunday, November 9th.* . . . I sat next the true Englishman again to my delight, he told me that in Poland if a lady thinks a gentleman too attentive to her daughter, and does not wish for the match, when he dines there a dish of black beans is served up, and he never dines there again. I don't see how the lady though can tell that he wishes to offer till he does the deed. . . .

"The Germans sat next Uncle, and were going to the opera. The beastly men before us began smoking before the ladies left, wretches! We asked the W——s to come and sit with us by our fire, which they did, and told us such stories of the love of dirt of the French. . . . A boy they had, when made to wash himself every morning, began crying, and said, 'Mais les Messieurs Français ne se lavent jamais qu'une fois pas semaine!' Others exclaimed, 'C'est si sale de ces Anglais, d'être toujours à se laver, se laver.' The common people do not think themselves in good health if they have not lice, and if they are without them by chance, they transplant them from those who have, to those who have not. I never heard such horrors in my life, my blood creebled.

"*Monday, November 10th.* . . . I sat next the nice Indian man, who nearly killed me with laughing by the most enthusiastic way in which he talked of the beauty of the English women. He is determined not to marry till he returns again from India three years hence, and partly the reason he came abroad was that if he stayed six months in England he should get married, and he will not do so till he leaves India, so he has put an 'iron plate all over his chest and heart' till he returns from India. I was excessively amused—he is worthy of being an Englishman to be so enthusiastic about England and all in it, as he is. Uncle and he got talking of India together, and I was quite sorry when it was time to go upstairs. . . ."

They started from Terni on Sunday, November 16.

"At half past six a good natured fille with a dagger to keep up her hind hair called me. . . . The road very ugly after the first ten miles, . . . those ten miles to me were delightful, so very like Berkshire, copse and underwood and hills like Highclere. . . . We saw St. Peter's at a long distance off, and passed Nero's tomb. . . . The eternal city looked indeed a most wonderful place, I little thought that my Roman history would ever be so interesting to me. We came through the gate or Porto del Popolo where a man got two pauls for professing to let us pass without an examination of things—he after all sent a soldier with us to the Albergo dell' Europe who expected to be feed or to search the things. Uncle determined to stand out and would not give a sou, so all our things were looked at, and in the search the little brooch Papa gave me was lost. I could have cried, but did not mention it. . . ."

CHAPTER III.

DIARY (*Continued*).

From Jane's journal written in Rome, we must give but brief extracts. The Eternal City, even as seen through the wide-awake eyes of a girl of sixteen, is too well known already. She was enthusiastic over the Colosseum, over pictures, over music, and heartily enjoyed taking singing lessons and seeing new sights and new people. We give only a short specimen of her comments on statues—more from the picture it brings of the little brother at home than for any artistic reason.

"*Monday, November 24th.* On our way to the picture gallery we passed through a hall filled with beautiful statues, &c., one of a boy just like Squab (Arthur), the fat pet! with his arms round a goose's neck, tugging away at it; so like what Squab does to old Nep! this delighted me as much as any, for it spoke to one's heart. . . ."

In Rome Jane hears for the first time, apparently, of the hideous cruelty shown to the Poles by Russia, and gives the following account. We wish it were the last of the sufferings of this unhappy people, but in 1916 we hear of far worse.

"*Tuesday, November 25th.* . . . Just before dinner Miss Kate M—— called. . . . She told me what if true is most horrid, that at some place in Poland the governor had tortured several nuns to *death* because they would not embrace the Greek Church and leave the Roman Catholic, and the Emperor of Russia had upheld him. Three or four nuns escaped, one of the abbesses who is now in Rome, has a dreadful cut across her forehead inflicted by the governor. The Emperor's treatment of the Poles is horrid still; he has all the children of the upper classes taken from the parents and married to the boors and booresses in Siberia. One poor princess had her eight children taken from her, one only six weeks old; she followed the cart containing them till she dropped dead. The ladies of Poland, when their husbands were sent to work in the Siberian mines, went with them like good angels (honours to our sex) and live with their husbands in wretched little huts. They are made to work in chains, the chains galled their legs, a petition was presented to the Emperor by the wives, that they might wear worsted stockings to prevent this, and it was refused. If these stories are true they make one's blood boil, that such a devil incarnate should have defiled England with his presence; but one cannot believe these stories, one will not believe all, at least, but if I were the Pope I would see the Emperor 'furder furst' before he should put his foot in Rome. . . .' "

We next give Jane's account of two expeditions, one a trip to the grotto of the Sibyl, and the other an inadvertent visit to a monastery.

"*Wednesday, November 26th.* Got up at six. Uncle performed lady's maid as the antique 'fille' sleeps out of the house. At a little after seven we finished breakfast, and were off in our private carriage behind two nice little horses. . . . The grotto of the Sibyl is

most wonderful and awful; slippery steps conduct
you down to a cavern, where on your left hand the
water comes rushing along from the old cascade, and
on your right it disappears down an awful looking
abyss with a tremendous noise. . . . We pursued our
way through beautiful shrubberies to the new cascade, the largest.   This fall was nearly as beautiful
as Terni. . . . If a person *will* commit suicide, why
does he not come here and do it in style?   It would
be some comfort dying in such an awfully beautiful
fall as this, instead of ending one's life miserably in
a dirty duck pond. . . . Got to the Hotel and had
dinner, at which 3 dogs and 2 cats, all nearly starved,
attended; fed them well. . . .

   "*Thursday, November 27th.* . . . We took a cab and
drove through the most extraordinary little streets
to the Campo Vaceino.   At the beginning of the ruins
we got out and walked, making for the palace of the
Cæsars. . . . We poked about, passed several cottages
between two walls, which hid the ruins of the palace
from our sight.   We came to two wooden gates,
pushed them open and continued our walk among old
pieces of stone and marble grown over with weeds.
Passing a gate looking more immediately upon the
site of the old palace, I looked through the key hole,
and discovered that they had turned the ground on
which the Emperors had trod into a cabbage garden,
and there was no way of roaming about among the
ruins better than we were then in.   I gathered some
wild flowers, and having come to a 'cul de sac' re-
traced our steps and found the gates shut and locked!
a blow.   I perceived another gate belonging to a
house close by unlocked, so made for it, opened it
and perceiving three monks, was beginning to ask
them to open the gate, when I was driven back by
their exclaiming, 'No! No! No! andate via! andate

via! no! no! no!' I was glad to 'andate via' as the
smell of garlic was considerable, and my Uncle then
stepped up and explained how we had wandered in;
though they had sent me away, they seemed to be
delighted to see me, poor old things! and I was laughing ready to kill myself at getting into a monastery!
They evidently wished to see the last of me, for they
all three went to open the gate, and seemed pleased
at my nodding with a broad grin and saying, 'addio,
addio.' . . ."

We give brief extracts describing two more oc-
currences in Rome. The first, the fixing of the date
of departure, gave Jane especial delight; the second,
a sight of a ceremony in the Sistine Chapel, caused her
a not too reverent amusement.

"*Sunday, December 7th.* At breakfast I was made
mad with joy. Uncle said we should only be here
three weeks more—till after Xmas!! Joy! Joy! . . .
The day was perfectly heavenly and our walk very
enjoyable. I saw the Miss Hays, the young man
they were talking with was smoking. In this public
walk, with ladies, it was bad taste I thought. . . .

"*Monday, December 8th.* . . . After breakfast went
to the Sistine Chapel. It was the feast of the concep-
tion of the Virgin. A little trouble to get in because
Uncle had not a straight cut coat. The same old
officer who got me in before got me a seat and allowed
Uncle to stand behind the Swiss guard. I had a good
look at the frescos. . . . The old Pope prayed, and he
has a very fine voice. They smothered him with
incense, and the way they bang the great cap on his
head is enough to break his neck. Then when he
sits down, half a dozen padres in purple pull down his
petticoats and arrange his clothes, just such a process
as mounting a lady on horseback. . . ."

We close Jane's diary at Rome with her account of one of the last days she spent there.

"*Tuesday, December 30th.* . . . At two Lady and Kate M—— called for me, and after getting a pair of white satin shoes, we went off to see the baths of Caracalla. . . . The old mosaic pavement quite perfect in some parts. Kate and I remonstrated at Lady M——'s ordering the servant to pick up some to take away. We then ascended the flight of steps leading to the top of the ruins, and went along some awful places, large holes on each hand. Lady M—— was very venturesome, poking her nose everywhere, and we were in agony for her, for she is as blind as a beetle. There is a very beautiful view from the top, but we were very glad to get down not only on our own account but on Lady M——'s, for some years ago she mistook a precipice for a path and jumped right down a declivity of near 30 feet. . . . Came home and dined at eight, went to the Burrough's. . . . The people came, dancing began, and my Uncle and a few others went to play whist. I first danced with a Mr. K——, a very amiable kind of a little man. . . . My next partner was a strange creature; he declared he had seen me last season in London, and would not believe I was not out; he told me in the first ten minutes that he was the most wretched of men, made me understand he had been crossed in love, told me he had once played very high and consequently now would never touch a card. Also he told me he was a fatalist, so (although I thought him joking) I told him my opinion and gave him good advice under a laughing exterior, for which advice he will care about as much as for last year's wind. But I could not help liking him for all that. My last partner was a little man who had got a fall at hunting. His arm was

much swelled, and he kept knocking it against
other people, which made him say 'the devil.'
After this I was tired, and my Uncle's whist over,
so we went.

"*Wednesday, December 31st.* Our last day in Rome.
. . . We went on the Pincean for a last look. . . . I
have spent a most happy seven weeks here, but how
happy I shall be to leave it for Home! Our friends
have all been most kind, but I am Home-sick and
mother-sick and father-sick, and brother-sick and
sister-sick. . . . I had a deal to do when we went to
bed, working and packing, and I had determined to
see the New Year in, for dear Tom and Fan were to be
looking on the stream, and listening to the Newberry
bells, while I was to listen to the Roman bells.

"*Thursday, January 1, 1846.* . . . After Catarina had
taken an affectionate leave of me by kissing my hand
(a process which she afterwards performed on Uncle
Tom) we got off. . . . The Campagna is more bleak
on this side than on the others, till one gets near
Civita Vecchia. The sea as smooth as a frozen pond,
and we passed through ground covered with bushes
of myrtle, azalea and broom. Fine herds of 'boves'
and goats, milk white goats, were feeding amongst
the bushes. The hotel Orlandi was a capital one;
we got charming rooms looking on the sea, and then
set out to walk, the hush of the sea and the voices
rising as distinctly as on a summer's evening—and
the beautiful green and purple of the sea, and the
sun getting low, all made me calmly, perfectly happy—
and the feeling that we were 50 miles towards home not
a little contributed to my joy."

They waited patiently for their steamer, the "Maria
Christina." On January 3 she was sighted, and on
the 4th they started. The next day they touched

Leghorn, and on the 6th arrived at Genoa. The following extracts are taken from her account of the voyage:—

"At dinner I eat some soup and beef with appetite but was not sorry then to escape with my Uncle to the deck. The evening was perfect. The sky red and gold with the sunset, the moon and stars bright and lovely, and the spray blowing in one's face. It was very hard to keep our legs, but we tumbled about till half past eight. I enjoyed it amazingly and did not feel the least sick. I brushed and undressed and got to bed and went fast asleep. (Next morning.) Turned out and did my hair. The poor ladies had not slept at all, but had been envying me. They kept exclaiming, 'you'll be very sick if you keep walking about so,' but I laughed, washed, dressed and was not sick. . . .

"*Monday, January 5th.* . . . The ladies went below; the husband of the darkest lady walked and talked with me and does not improve with acquaintance. He talked of the foreign men, and he was excessively curious to find out (as I admired Englishmen) if I was engaged. I thought his pumping rude, so at last after bearing and warding off his questions, I told him I was 17—and then turned the subject; but he returned to it, would not believe my age, and began saying that religion and love were incompatible. I told him I utterly disapproved of his opinions, and that nothing could convince me that love could be happy without being based, supported, and entirely influenced by religion, and then asked if he was not afraid of the night air with his cough; so he went below to my joy. . . . [At dinner] he and Uncle talked politics; he is quite on the wrong side, and he is a bit of a horse-dealer, and a 'leg' I fancy—runs

horses and bets on them—poor man though! I fear
he is not long for this world, he has a sad cough. . . ."

At Genoa she passed the "ever-to-be-remembered
post-office" where she had received the note from her
brother Tom which had sent her mad with joy. The
next day they continued their journey.

"We left by the way we entered from the Corniche
last time. The day was very bright but bitterly cold—
icicles hanging from the rocks five or six feet long,
and even running streams frozen up. The road wound
in and out among high hills, parched with frost, as
brown as possible, with a frozen stream at the base—
a most singular and wild drive. The sun was getting
low and I saw the Alps for the first time, an immense
way off—most lovely they looked. The colour of the
sky was glorious. I slept a little when it grew darker
and woke coldish—such a hard frost, and a beautiful
moon. We got to Alessandria about 7. Went to
bed early—read in bed till I drove away the blue
devils with those splendid Psalms of David.

"*Thursday, January 8th.* Up at six—breakfast and
off at half past seven. Such a bitter morning, I never
saw such a frost. We shut up the carriage, and the
windows were frozen over in no time. The post-boy's
breath and Giovanni's froze on their comforters. . . .
The Alps looked splendid, the sun shining on their
snowy tops. . . .

"*Friday, January 9th.* Got off at last—left Turin by
an avenue six miles long. . . . The sun set splendidly—
there was a slight mist half way up the hills and the
colours of the sunset reflected on it! Then the moon
rose, and the effect of that with the deep blue sky
sprinkled with stars beyond, will never escape my
memory. By the time we got to Susa I was in a state

of frenzy—I never felt so before. I never enjoyed a
ride or rather a drive as I did this, it was magnificent—
glorious. How little it makes one feel, and how Great
and how Good He who placed these mountains. We
went to the Hotel della Posta—got a good fire and
dinner. At half past eight went to bed; fire in my
room—sat up late by it thinking of the dear ones in
England.

"*Saturday, 10th January.* Started at half past seven
for M. Cenis. . . . At the summit is a post house, and
while we were changing horses we eat some of our
loaf, and drank some of the half bottle of white
Hermitage. I drank the health of all the dear ones
in England individually and collectively. . . . The sun
set and the red light was as beautiful as ever, just
tinging the tops till very late, and then the moon
began shining, and I never saw anything so beautiful.
We entered a wild, wild valley, very narrow with
immense high mountains on each side—one side in
shade all except the very summits, whose snowy tops
the moon was shining on—all the other side was in
clear light, like the day, everything perfectly distinct.
By our side rushed the Isere over its rock bed, the
snow shone brighter than diamonds with all the
prismatic colours. It was a sight I never can forget,
and there was an awfulness about it which though
pleasing for one night would have been painful for
more. We saw a fox. . . . We got on to 'Grande
Maison' to sleep, a solitary post house where we got a
very good supper between 8 and 9. It was a bitter
cold night, but for all that I could not get to bed
but sat up looking out of window at the moon on the
snow mountains, and thinking of England as usual
till I was perfectly petrified.

"*Sunday, January 11th.* . . . We left 'Grande Maison'
at half past seven. . . . Beyond les Echelles there is a

most awful pass, one goes along the brink of a precipice thousands of feet below and above you, a river at bottom, and nothing, not even a parapet to prevent your looking into the awful depths below! where the river was dashing along like mad, and the road was giving way on all sides, and was so narrow, and if two things had met, one must have backed for a mile at least. The Corniche was nothing to this. I was most thankful to be out of it. . . . At the Hotel de la Posta we got a good dinner and beds, and I had a fire in my room, and did not I just sit up and look at the embers till Heaven knows what o'clock, thinking of Home! but I felt ill, and not inclined to go to bed, and got a pain in my chest; I had been drinking too much wine, for the day I came over M. Cenis I drank more wine than I had done the whole time I had been in Italy, for I had only drank one glass then and coming over M. Cenis I had two good pulls at the bottle. At last I went to bed and slept very badly."

Jane's reasoning would have pleased a temperance reformer—her illness all due to her terrible excesses of the day before, and not to sitting up late on "a bitter cold night" "thinking of England" till she was "perfectly petrified."

The next day she writes:—

"*Monday, January 12th.* Started about eight. I could not eat any breakfast, had a horrid headache, and was very sick, with a dreadful pain in my chest. Nothing could exceed my Uncle's kindness, had he been my mother or a husband he could not have taken more care of me, and took off his own comforter to wrap me in, and cosseted me dreadfully. How very grateful I am to him, for his kindness to me in bringing me abroad and in taking such kind care of me! . . . Spent the evening in writing journal, &c., and finished my letter to Mama. Went to bed in my wee bedroom—got in a dreadful funk because my chest ached badly, but got to bed and rubbed it well, and read till I was sleepy the Psalms, then in my dressing gown and in a most comfortable bed, I went to sleep."

She doesn't mention feeling ill the next day, and seems to have recovered, for she went to see the sights of Lyons. She mentions a high wind blowing!

Before they left Lyons she notes:—

"My Uncle had Giovanni up to discharge him, he is now too bad; he is civil enough to me and does anything for me, but he does not like my Uncle, never is punctual and is twice as much bother as use."

They spent the following night at Roanne, and left early the next day, January 15. They travelled all that day, all that night, and the next day. She writes of the journey as follows:—

"With the exception of the south part of the country, France is anything but 'belle,' barren downs, straggling villages, trees with all their branches lopped off for firewood—in short, bleak and dismal to an awful degree. . . . We had such roads as I never yet saw or imagined—I thought we never should get through them; they were regular 'sloughs of despond'—steep hills, with the road like ploughed fields from the thaw— the 'cantonniers' too have a clever way of making them worse; they put a stone as big as an English household loaf into a rut two feet deep and cover it up with watery mud! consequently the roads get worse and worse, and the carriage wheels get into the

holes, and one fancies they will never get out—but
the 'Incomparable' as we have named the little carriage stood it all bravely and I will defy any one to
find her equal. We stopped at about four at a place
called 'Varennes' at the wee 'Hôtel de la Poste' to
dine. . . . Left well refreshed for our night's travelling.
I very soon went to sleep though it was so early.
We got to Moulins about eleven—moon beautiful—
a very warm night. The postilions go capitally at
night, and though they are always 'bien endormi'
when one arrives, they are not long turning out.
Poor Uncle got a bad cold again and did not sleep. . . .

"Both my Uncle and myself were dead sick of post-
ing. My legs twitched, and I could hardly sit still, and
I had to keep comforting myself by thinking, 'Well, we
are on our way home, every step I am nearer Donnington. Tomorrow for the railroad—adieu to postilions
after to-day.' We entered Orléans about half past
eight. We went to Hôtel d'Orléans near the railroad,
got some tea and went to bed. Had not I just a
wash! and brush! I did not get to bed till past one
—but I was clean when I did get there and did I not
sleep?"

The next day they went by train, having duly had
the carriage put on board. Of her journey to Paris,
she records:—

"Opposite me sat an old gentleman who kept
fidget-fidget with his legs close by mine, till I was
nearly out of my senses—but I stowed myself at last so
that I did not feel his movements although he kept
beating the devil's tattoo the whole way, and without
intending to be impudent he had such a grin on his
countenance whenever our eyes happened to meet
that I was obliged to turn one side to him and not

look at him.   If I had not done so I must have laughed,
for he was so like a good-humoured cod-fish. . . . I
lolled back, thought what delightful things railroads
were.   We were four hours coming from Orléans to
Paris, and arrived at half past two.   Got the carriage
off, and had post horses to take us into Paris."

On Sunday, January 18, Jane attended church to
her great satisfaction.   On Monday she gives the
following account:—

"... The washerwoman came, and then my Uncle
courier-ised the carriage, which was to be ready by
four to be in time for the train at five.   At four all
was ready, the horses had been ordered at the railroad of the 'commis' for four, and they did not come till
ten minutes to five.   Little M. Meurice came scuttling
up the stairs to me, but I had seen the horses come
before he got half way up, and knocked him down
nearly.   When we got to the train they refused to
put the carriage on, saying it was too late—the little
'commis' was rushing about and declaring it was
'trop tard, trop tard,' and was inclined to be impudent
till my Uncle showed him there was one John Bull who
could speak French and manage without a courier.
My Uncle declared he would 'enregistrer' and complain
to the directors that the little 'commis' had not sent
the horses till half an hour after he had ordered them,
and when the fat little button of a man heard this, he
turned very pale, got very civil, and was in a precious
funk.   'Il faut mettre la voiture,' said my Uncle,
dodging the poor little 'commis' round a pillar where
he was trying to hide himself.   'Mais monsieur,' said
the little 'commis' perspiring with fright for fear any
of the directors should hear of his neglect.   'Je vous
dis qu'il faut mettre la voiture.'   'Mais M.! si vous

voulez donc partir avec cette convoie.' 'Mais la
voiture.' 'Ah, M., si vous voulez bien partir, je payerai
tout, postilion, voiture, tout!' Nothing was heard but
'si vous voulez partir' and 'la voiture' and I sat in the
carriage in fits of laughter, watching my Uncle chase
the fat little 'commis,' and at last they got out of sight,
and I lay back and thought, 'well, whilst my Uncle
writes and complains to the directors, I can have a two
hour nap, for the next train goes at seven.' When all
at once I heard a great scuffling and shouting of
'descendez! descendez Madame! descendez! par ici.'
Out I jumped, saw the little 'commis' more excited than
ever, panting and puffing and trying to run before me
to the train. I guessed the truth, that my Uncle had
consented to go by this train, and to have the carriage
sent by the next, the little 'commis' being answerable
for all the things, and paying all. So feeling that at
the commis' quickest pace I should never reach the
train before it started, I pushed him aside and showed
him how an English girl could run!! outstripping him
by ages and arriving three seconds before the train
started. We had then a good laugh over the excite-
ment of the little 'commis'—I never saw anything more
rich than the whole scene. There were three Frenchmen in the train, or rather in the carriage with us;
'commis voyageur' kind of fellows—the one opposite
me very good natured, and I talked to him to improve
my French. Of course he told me I spoke very well,
that is a regular bit of 'blarnie Française.' . . . They
asked me if there was any society in the country, and
if at English balls there were musicians or whether the
ladies played, whether the English could dance, and if
the young people enjoyed gayety. . . . We passed
through a tunnel or two. The Frenchmen were in
an agony of fright; the one opposite me—who by the
bye had a basket lined with fur for his feet—let down

the glass in the cold draughty tunnel, and poking his head out of the window, examined the brick work most anxiously—pulling in his head, he called across to the other two, who were examining the other side. 'C'est sec! c'est bien sec.' 'Oui, oui, c'est bien sec! c'est bien fait, cela ne tombera pas je crois.' By this time Uncle Tom and I were quite cold—I got a cold in my head which went next day, so was of no consequence. We got to Rouen at nine, and went in a bus to the Grand Hôtel de Rouen, and got tea.''

The next day (the 20th), they went from Rouen to Dieppe, and at half-past four on the 21st they embarked on the "Menai" for England. Jane was "absolutely sea-sick" on the voyage, but cured herself with a "captain's biscuit." When on shore she walked to Shoreham, while her uncle was detained in the custom-house. She writes:—

"We got to the Star Inn, and sent off post horses to the Custom-House to my Uncle, and got Mrs. Cross, the jolly old landlady of the Star, to lend me dry shoes, and then I got the rooms comfortable, and waited anxiously for Uncle Tom, a coal fire and a poker being my companions; but I could not believe that I was in England, really in the dear tight little Island where my heart had been, and thoughts had been, for the last four months. . . .

"*Thursday, January 22nd.* Got off to go the mile to the train close to where we landed, behind English post horses, *leather* traces and clean harness. . . . Got into a queer little office to wait for the train while Uncle looked after the 'Incomparable,' and the 'Haricots.' I was quite *charmed* to hear a jolly Jack Tar talking in a *true* broad English and saying a '*biler*' had *busted*.'

... Directly we got out of the hilly downs close to Brighton, the fields looked delightful, so different to the uncultivated or weedy wastes abroad. Every field in England is like a *garden*, not a weed to be seen! What a glorious country this is! ... While my Uncle got the carriage off I sat in the waiting-room and we soon got for the last time into the dear little 'Incomparable,' and rolled off through *dear* London. ... We went to Morley's in Trafalgar Square. ... After dinner I wrote to Grandmama, Uncle slept; he was quite tired with his *courier* acting, and no wonder. ... I thought of Home. (At four saw the Senior's 'van' as Min calls it and Mrs. Senior's pelisse pass.)

"*Friday, January 23d.* ... We sallied forth, he to the city on business, I to Grandmama's in a cab. Found Grandmama looking very well. ... We talked over my going home, and a young Mr. Vincent called, some fifth cousin or other who was going to Oxford next day, and kindly offered to take me in charge. I look much more able to take care of him than he of me, I being three times as big as he is, and I intend to say that I saw Mr. Vincent safe to Reading, and forwarded him on by train to Oxford. Seriously though, it is most kind of him to take me, for he will have to wait an hour alone at Reading for his gallantry."

The next day she went home as planned. She writes:—

"Talked of churches in Normandy to good little Vincent, but when that was exhausted I thought I must astonish him so talked wildly of balls, &c. ...

"Mama met me at the Pelican. Was there ever happiness like mine then? The little boys were with her. At Home the first people were Tom and dear Fan looking perfectly happy—Papa, George, John,

Margaret.* I could not sleep for joy, to think that I am at home at dear, dear Donnington.

"So farewell old book! You have been a good friend and listened patiently to all my stupidities for the last three months, and I love you, and shall take care of you all my life, and often think of you with gratitude, for by telling you how dull I felt, I often have relieved myself. So I am almost sorry to say goodbye to you, although I shall not quite cut you, but frequently renew my acquaintance with you, so again Goodbye old fellow."

* Margaret Wilkinson, her cousin.

CHAPTER IV.

DIARY OF WALTER SCOTT HUGHES.

We here turn from Jane's diary to the journal written by her brother, Walter Hughes. We need scarcely apologise for introducing a sketch of one who was so bound up with the brightest recollections of her girlhood.

According to family tradition, Walter was the most joyous and gallant of all the brothers,—a tall, lithe figure, six foot one in his socks, broad-shouldered and thin-flanked. He was the hero of his younger brother Hastings, whom he sometimes used to honour by taking him on fishing expeditions and letting him handle the gaff. It was the greatest tragedy of the small boy's life that he once lost a fine fish his brother had nearly landed. "The worst thing about it was," he used to say, "that Walter never said a reproachful word. If only he had licked me, I should have felt better!"

Like Tom Brown, Walter left behind him at school "the name of a fellow who never bullied a little boy or turned his back on a big one." At Woolwich he did more, and stood out with two or three others against some abuses, winning thereby the admiration of his family and the disapproval of those of his superiors who did not wish to have the affair exposed.

We have a diary of Walter's, written originally in a

voluminous blank book, and sandwiched in between poems, anecdotes, accounts of military campaigns, receipts for fish-bait and flies, and prescriptions for horses. He probably placed more importance on noting that a horse's appetite might be stimulated with "warm ale and ginger" than on writing any of the incidents of his own life. Yet this is almost the only record we have of Jane's favourite brother and so-called twin, and we give parts of it in order that this memoir of her may be, in some sort, a memoir of him also.

EXTRACTS FROM JOURNAL OF WALTER SCOTT HUGHES.

When I was eight years old I went to school at R. Wickham's of Twyford, where I remained a year, after which to Rugby, where I was for a year and a half under Dr. Arnold. . . . I was soon after this offered a nomination to the R. M. Academy at Woolwich which was accepted for me; the nomination was offered by the Duke of Sussex. On this I went to J. R. Milhn, Esq., a preparatory school for the R. M. A. and here I remained for 3½ years till December, 1840. I passed my entrance examination to the R. M. A. in February, 1841, second [in a class of 12]. . . . The examinations for Commission took place Dec., 1843—the mathematical examiner, desiring to save himself trouble, had been in the habit of giving a certain course of papers in rotation. This was discovered and taken advantage of by some of those under examination, and as I could not work up beforehand, questions which were to be given as an *examination*, I did not obtain the place I desired, being 13th. . . .

I returned to the R¹ Arsenal, Woolwich, to study

for a half year the practical part of my profession,
and was appointed to the Artillery *June 18,** 1844,
a glorious day for obtaining a commission. I made a
short tour on the continent immediately after this,
of which the following are the particulars:

June 29, 1844. The packet started at 9 o'clock
from London Bridge. . . . Got to Ostend at half past
eleven. . . . [Lawler and Clarke, travelling companions.]

June 30. Got to Bruges by 6. . . . The tour
de Bruges is a large and very high building and at
the top a belfry of 47 bells, said to be the finest in
Europe. They are almost continually playing, and
sound prettily enough when one is at a distance from
them; but the effect was stunning on our ascending the
tower and getting close to them. They are played by
large wooden keys the same as a pianoforte. I
desired very much to give the neighbourhood a treat
in the way of "God Save the Queen" and had commenced operations, when the musician informed me
that as I was performing evolutions hardly consistent
with the air (but which no doubt might have been
taken for variations) it would be better to cease, thus
the populace was cheated of their treat. . . .

July 2. Ghent. . . . One thing I forgot to mention
which being peculiar to foreign countries ought to be
mentioned: in the churches, on each side of the priest's
reading desk we saw boxes 2 ft. by 1, filled with a
flowery substance for the officiating priest to spit in!!!!
. . . Clarke and Lawler went to the ball, and I came
home to write my journal as I hate balls where one
knows no one and is obliged to *dress.* . . .

July 8th. Started for Namur [from Brussels] by
half past four train; got there by half past eight.
Walked round the town; the people were holding a

* Waterloo.

kind of fair, there were several shows, &c. We entered
one and had the pleasure of seeing what is called a
giantess, but in reality a girl of 19 fed to an immense
extent of obesity with a leg like an elephant, and rolls
of fat under her chin sufficient to serve London in
tallow for a month. . . .

July 9.   Started by steamboat at 3 in the afternoon
for Liège. . . . I added on this day a most unique
article to my sketches in the shape of a little priest
possessing the most ludicrous countenance by far
that I have ever set eyes on; he was an usher to a
pack of school boys in blouses, who were travelling
by the boat. As I was sketching him, taking great
care not to allow him to see what I was about, Clarke
looked over my shoulder and then at his face to remark the likeness, and the little man thus found out
my object and commenced telling his pupils all kinds
of raw-head and bloody-bones stories about the bar-
barous (! ! !) and ever-to-be-hated English, at which
we laughed heartily, but those relations appeared
strongly to affect the minds of his hearers with horror
and dread of our countrymen which they showed by
their sidelong looks at us. . . .

July 11.   I spent the day seeing the town (Liège).
Museum, University, heads of animals in pickle—
nice kind of provision in case of a siege. . . .

July 16.   Started by the same boat at 6 A.M. [up
the Moselle]. . . . Arrived at Thier or Treves at 4
P.M.   Raining very hard, in spite of which we went
to see the lions of the oldest city in Germany—first
to the church of Notre Dame, the interior of which
is of very beautiful architecture and pleased us much;
there is also a very fine painting by Guido; we went
out of this into the cloisters of the old Monastery and
from thence through a door into the cathedral; our
Commissioner, without any announcement, opened the

sacristan's door; we entered the room; and after waiting a little time during which there was a slight scuffling in the inner chamber, the sacristan came out looking a little excited and proceeded to show us some splendid manuscripts, relics, &c.; imagining that neither Lawler nor myself knew anything of German he addressed our Commissioner, who appeared to be a crony of his, in the same manner as if they had been alone, and the conversation he carried on was rather amusing. To us in French: "This Messieurs is the gospel according to St. Mark, a manuscript of the 7th century written in these cloisters by a very holy man." To the Commissioner in German: "The devil take you, Hans, what do you bring visitors in here for, in such a hurry and without any announcement and Me, the holy sacristan, drinking brandy and water." To us: "This Messieurs is the skull of St. Helen, and beside it the skull of St. Matthew." To the Commissioner: "A nice story they'd have had to tell their friends, and then the Holy Church would have been in good repute, had you brought them into the inner room, you blockhead. The servants of the Holy Church can enjoy no comfort without interruption." . . . A lot of Prussian soldiers came in [to the Hotel] to sup and enjoy themselves for the evening. They appear jolly fellows with very large capacities for that most stomach-torturing-gripes-in-the-morning liquid, they call beer; when all trades fail in England and I am obliged to go abroad to live, I shall set up a large brewery of the *right sort*, in Germany; and if it does not answer, darn my old stockings. . . .

July 17. We started down the Moselle by the same packet. . . . Our dinner on board was a good general specimen of a German dinner so I shall give the bill of fare,—Soup, or rather greasy water in which meat has been boiled with chopped vegetables therein; the

meat which has made this same water greasy and with
well cooked vegetables, French mustard (a great
luxury) and sauces to give it a relish; cutlets, made
dishes in variety—fish with hot oil or something that
looks like it, I was told that this was melted butter
and that they don't put flour in it, which gives it this
appearance—half done ham, very salt, cut in thin
small slices, and looking like raw bacon exactly, and
pickled herrings cut in small slices without any accom-
paniment (faugh!) this is to make me thirsty and
give a zest to the appetite—(Here's a follower!) Light
pudding with rich fruit sauce and other sweets, tan-
tadlings, &c. (Here the uninitiated Englishman lolls
back in his chair, parts his waistcoat and thinking he
has done very well, feels for his toothpick); deluded
mortal, if you desire to keep in countenance the still
hungry natives around you, you must quietly insert
your digits under your coat tails and let a reef, aye
a large reef, out of your already tightened don't-talk-
about-ems, for lo! heralded by a goodly savour,
approach the very staff of the slight midday repast,
viz a very large joint of boiled beef, dº of roast mutton,
a goose and a couple of chickens, and a salad that
would even send Sydney Smith into fits, and if thou
wouldst follow the customs of the country, of each
and all these thou must partake of a goodly allowance
—Dessert, cakes, &c., &c. . . .

July 28. (Ostende) Bathed and was nearly carried
out to sea by ebb tide—men and women *all* together;
obliged on account of this *beastly* practice (for I saw
no *pretty* woman) to bathe in a jacket and bathing
trousers which was nearly the cause of my being scum-
fished. Started for England at 9 A.M. Got there by
½ p. 3.

My family at home were of course astonished to
see me, having returned earlier than they expected.

I joined at Woolwich the first of September, oh unhappy mortal. I got a strain on horse-back the
beginning of October and was ill a month at Woolwich, then going on sick leave I remained till the 7th
of January when I took Rugby in my way to Woolwich (rather roundabout) and never spent a pleasanter
week in my life. . . . Amongst other amusements we
got up charades and managed them pretty well and
as it was my "first appearance on any stage whatever"
the novelty was a great recommendation, and besides
this there was not one there who did not always desire
to be pleased however poor the attempt. . . . Another
of our amusements was singing glees, catches, rounds,
&c., &c. We had 6 voices, 3 ladies, 3 gentlemen, and
till I went to Rugby I never knew the *real pleasure* to
be derived from music, singing in particular. All
that's bright must fade, and the time came for me to
join at Woolwich and verily the contrast was such
as to make me doubly value the happenings I had so
lately enjoyed. I did duty at Woolwich till April when
my old complaint showed again, and now I am writing
on the third of May after having been ill one month.
I go on sick leave again tomorrow and almost fear
that the authorities will think I am shirking; they
will be very far from the point, however, but it is
very likely as they love me not. My sister Jeanie
and my mother are at Hastings' and I go there to
them; poor Jeanie is there for her health. Poor girl!
it is an affection of one of her lungs. Please God it may
not become worse.

May 4, Sunday. Waited patiently for my leave
till about 4 P.M. when I got it at last and started immediately for New Cross and from thence by railway to
Staplehurst where I slept the night. (May 5) started
next morning per coach to Hastings' where I arrived
at about ½ p. 3, found my mother and sister at the

Marine Hotel, poor Jeanie very ill; with an ear ache into the bargain. Took a warm bath at 96° Faht . delicious! ! !

May 6. Got up early at about 7, walked out on the beach—windy day and cold—returned in an hour. My mother and Jeanie dreadfully lazy and did not get up till 10. Shrimps and bread and butter! ! ! . . .

May 8. . . . Dined early as usual. After dinner Jeanie, Ben and self took a sail; sea rough, shipped lots of water but through the intervention of the sailor's "hoil cloak" Jeanie was not touched by a drop. Spite of the motion Jeanie and self stood it well, my sister being the more delighted, the greater the swell; . . . Read Miss Austen's "Sense and Sensibility." She makes people in apparently high life talk and act vulgarly in some cases, and takes rather an uncomfortable view of the *men*. There is not *one decently* first rate male, while Elinor and Marianne are delightful (this is perhaps the reason the women like the book!), . . . Edward is slow and irresolute in some things and Col. Brandon a muff for not shooting Willoughby or being shot after he *had* called him out, which is the Rubicon of duelling.

May 9. Went out with Jeanie fishing after breakfast. Jeanie and the sailor caught nothing but dogfish which are uneatable. I caught a Robin Hurle and several gurnets. Just as we pulled up our lines the last time Jeanie redeemed her credit by catching the finest gurnet we had caught.

May 10. . . . Got our piano. Commenced learning "Che faro sensa Euridice" from "Orpheus," a beautiful thing. . . .

May 13. . . . Major Bonamy* whom we expected

* (Afterwards) Colonel Bonamy who had been engaged to Mrs. Hughes' sister Dorothea. She died, and he never married. He was a constant visitor at the Hughes' house, and made great pets of the children.

arrived at tea-time—a most agreeable man. A *little* afraid I *fancy* of people thinking him *oldish*, and so *works it off* by affecting to be older than he really is —one of the most *sensible* men I know; (this is a large share of one's good opinion after reading Miss Austen's book, "Sense and Sensibility").

May 14. Jeanie and I went out for a sail whilst my mother and the Major took a long walk into the country. . . .

May 17. Dead calm. Jeanie, Emma and self fished. . . .

May 24. . . . I went sailing in the afternoon with Jeanie, Ford and Emma. Saw lots of birds because we had no gun.

Sunday 25. . . . Tea tête-à-tête, Jeanie. . . .

May 29. Read "Pride and Prejudice," capital book; but some parts overdrawn, which one expects in every novel. I hardly think that such insulting pride as Darcy's could be combined with such *perfect* goodness of heart, at least I have never seen it, and expect I never shall. Elizabeth and Jane are two very good characters, the former especially and exceedingly well drawn. The feeling of gratification in finding that a thoroughly proud and haughty man loved her is, I think, not expressed, and in the particular circumstances I fancy she must have slightly felt it. A woman I think would like to feel her power over a man, as yet quite unhumbled. . . .

June 2. . . . Went to the Lover's Seat with my mother and Jeanie. Calm evening, eat oysters with William Mann off the rocks. Jeanie, self and Ford went fishing and caught naught. . . .

The rest of the time at Hastings' passed pretty much this way. . . .

Saturday the 14th. Started for Woolwich per coach early in the morning, arrived there in the evening;

the old place going on pretty much as usual. We used to have during the short time I remained there, drill every morning at 6 with the Battery, and practice every day in the marshes or on the common. . . .

June 29. In orders that I am exchanged from Major Freen's Comp^y Halifax to Cap. Tylden's Company, Clonmel, Ireland—here's a go.

June 30. Bombadier of 9th Battery comes to ask me if I am ready to go to Ireland—reply, as soon as ever they wish and leave nothing much I regret. Went to see Sir Hew Ross to ask about going. He gives me to the 15th to get to Clonmel so I cut back to my room, pack up my portmanteau, leave Kirk in charge of everything and responsible to bring everything with him when he goes to Clonmel, and off I go to Donnington; just got in time for the four o'clock train. Donnington at ½ p. 7. . . .

July 1. Go out fishing near the house towards Shaw, middling sport—father returns in the evening, sing duets and glees with cousin Margery and Annie.*

July 2. . . . Hear from Jeanie and John who are again at Hastings'. . . .

[*Clonmel.*] *August 1st.* . . . Dressed and repaired to Dr. Shiels' evening party; we arrived happily at that time in the evening between the ladies retiring and the gentlemen joining them, an auspicious period but not taken proper advantage of by the ladies who sat the whole way round the room in chairs placed close together conversing entirely with one another and taking advantage of no opportunity to allow the gentlemen (Ford, Stark and self) to have a chance; I espied the prettiest Miss Shiels half way down stairs in a sort of sanctum sanctorum, 3 feet by 6, behind a table dealing out coffee; I immediately made a movement and ensconced myself by her side, found her very

* Margaret and Anne Wilkinson.

amusing, infinitely ladylike, and with the very slightest taste of the brogue which gave to whatever she said a charming piquancy; blonde is she, with such eyes. She has no "Baby Blake-ishness" whatever; has plenty to say for herself; is very open and speaks quickly with no rattle or affectation; she is, alas, one of *many* children; it's a sad pity she has not 50,000.£, and is not desperately attached to me. I must mind what I am about; there'd be the devil to pay if I was to fall in love with a girl; and as if old Nick were in it she happens to be just the right age although she appears almost grown up; what a capital thing keeping a journal is, it makes one expose and weigh one's inward remarks made previously, but not yet embodied in thought, perhaps from an innate dislike to do so, perhaps from negligence. I danced a good many times and was much amused. ... Old Shiels is a thorough trump—wanted me to sing but I could not think of such a thing among such a lot of perfect strangers, would have been ra-e-ther too much of an exhibition; he hinted about coming to practice when they were alone; this was just what I wanted and had been trying for the greater part of the time he had talked to me. I must improve this acquaintance— one of my chief sources of happiness is to be on familiar terms with some agreeable family where there are girls; and who are musical. N.B. There are three Miss Shiels so there is no chance of my tiring; variety is pleasant and indeed necessary for a poor subaltern with 200 a year and 9 cwts. of worldly goods and chattels. ...

Sunday, 3rd. Went to church, all respectable people are in the gallery, all the officers put in two pews; saw a good many of my friends of Friday night, Miss Bereton and the Shiels blooming. ...

Monday. Called on the Shiels, found eldest Miss Shiels singing "When Huther's Lips," etc. ...

Wednesday. . . . Went to Dr. Shiels' with another (Fenton), where the Dr. and Ford afterwards joined us; I spent a very pleasant quiet evening partly because the old lady and girls made themselves very agreeable and partly because they attempted to allow me to do the same, by singing, too, which is always an agreeable occupation.

Thursday. Started soon after 6 to Lismore with Forde and old Condon, the fisherman, &c., &c., in a jaunting car; we followed the course of the Suir for about 3½ miles and then turned off to the left up a very pretty glen; we continued along this for about five miles as far as Newcastle, a small and dirty village, but prettily situated on the Suir under the mountains; we had thus cut off a very long angle of the river; after baiting the horse we started up the mountain; to the left the road is cut in the side of the hill and is of the worst description, in some places it has fallen away and the wheel of the car passed within half a foot of a precipice about 200 ft. deep. The inhabitants were very busy getting in their turf for the winter's fire and long strings of carts with horses of a wretched description, but some showing good blood, were toiling their way up the mountain; we saw one remarkably pretty girl among them; the women assist in this work apparently very readily. They are indeed a light-hearted set, for except from their ragged habiliments one would little imagine the author of those well put jokes and ringing laughter to be in the lowest stage of poverty and distress, hardly knowing how he shall put bread into the mouths of himself and family. The road down the other side of the mountain was comparatively good, the only disagreeable part being the water-courses which cross the road about every fifty yards; they are paved with rough stones and are about half a foot deep

and the car gives a tremendous jolt in going over
them, for which if you are not prepared, you stand
a good chance of being precipitated headlong from
your perilous position. We arrived at the beautiful
Lismore at about 12, and after eating a hasty luncheon
we repaired to the river side. On coming to Lismore
we encountered a Mr. Johnstone and his friend Mr.
Hamilton, whom Ford had known previously. They
told us they had been at Lismore 10 days and had
not caught a single fish; however, I had hardly been
fishing ten minutes when I hooked a fine salmon who,
after showing about a quarter of an hour's good sport,
was safely gaffed by old Condon who was in high glee,
exclaiming, "Sure it was not 10 days we were here
without killing a salmon"; however, we caught no
more that evening, merely getting two or three good
rises; we returned to the inn and after dinner tried
again without success and after that went to bed.

Friday, August 8th. Rainy morning. Ford ad-
journed after breakfast to the castle promising he
would join us almost immediately; we saw directly
that there was no use at all trying the fly so we put
on the worm and tried in the stream about 300 yards
below the castle; I had hardly fished 10 minutes when
I got two runs but neither took—perhaps I was a
little too eager; presently, however, I got hold of a
fine fellow who spun out about 50 yards of my line in
a jiffy and rushed over the rapids below the hole.
However, after 20 minutes' play I landed him and he
was as beautifully formed a fish as I have ever seen,
but only weighed 7 lbs. . . .

Wednesday. Grouse shooting begins—devil a grouse
for one with rheumatism and ophthalmia. . . .

Sunday, 24th. Go to church—looks quite empty—
no ladies—dreadful—walked with young Shiels down
river. . . .

Dec. 21st, and I have written nothing at all. Jeanie has been making a tour of France and Italy with Uncle Tom and has been greatly amused; her mind is developing wonderfully under such good influences and I expect she will be much improved by the time she returns; my mother has kindly sent me all her letters which are very long and equally amusing. . . .

The diary of Walter Hughes stops here. The abrupt ending will leave us forever in doubt whether, as he patronisingly suggests, he found his sister's "mind wonderfully developed " and she herself "much improved" when they next met. Neither shall we ever read the letters from her which he found so amusing. If they were saved at the time, they must have been among those which were burned on that far-away hearth in Tennessee. Of Walter's subsequent history we know this much: that, all resolutions to the contrary, he lost his heart to Charlotte Shiels, that he became engaged to her, and that soon afterwards he was ordered to British Guiana. There he got malaria while fishing on one of the rivers. He recovered from this first attack, but the lure of his favourite sport was too strong for him. With youthful recklessness he went off on another fishing trip; he died of the second attack of fever then contracted.

JOHN HUGHES.

(From a crayon sketch, taken about 1830.)

CHAPTER V.

WALTER'S DEATH—FAMILY LETTERS.

Jane's diary introduced us to January, 1846, but we have no further accounts of that eventful year. Walter probably came home on furlough before starting for South America; Tom was engaged to Miss Frances Ford, the "dear Fan" of the diary; and Jane became engaged to Mr. Nassau Senior, the son of an old friend of her father's. Things went on in their usual round at Donnington, with the archery meeting and the hunt ball, with little boys home from school, and big boys back on vacations, and plenty of friends to enjoy the hum of young life and glad promise which pervaded the house. The family circle was still unbroken. None of the seven brothers had as yet made homes of their own, none had travelled so far but that they might some day be welcomed back, and the only sister was still there to gladden all eyes and hearts.

Into the midst of this wholesome and happy family life came, like a bolt from the blue, the news of Walter's death. He had been recovering from his first attack of fever when the last tardy post from Guiana had arrived. The next vessel brought tidings that he was dead, after a two days' illness. Hastings was sent to carry the news to the old grandmother. He was elated in the midst of his genuine grief at being intrusted with such an important mission. "Little beast that I was!" he used to say.

After the first shock, the family began to struggle for acquiescence and cheer. Jane was again taken ill, and her mother carried her to Ventnor for the sea air, while her father took charge of Henry and Arthur at home. It was during this time that he wrote the following letters to his wife. In the midst of their formal expression, one may read the strong feeling which he was unwilling to put into emotional words, even to her.

DEAREST MARGARET:—

I can now tell you that we are alive and well. I shall start on Saturday next; all the boys' things will be ready.

It is now high time to come, I begin to think I can be of use in keeping up your spirits, and I want your society. The worst is over with me and I have accustomed myself to look the thing composedly in the face; but I find a loathing of every day pursuits is coming over me, and feel bothered in this comparatively big house. Nothing can be more kindly and teachable than the two little men, both of whom I shall bring, but in fact I want grown people to talk of graver things; above all, yourself and I wish to see how you are in health.

Yours, etc.

About this time (1847) he writes again to his wife:—

. . . You know my notions habitually are that the church is not called the church militant without due reason, . . . so that if one's temperament includes . . . a tolerable share of moral and physical nerve, one's

vocation is to go at once up to the worst and fight it
down, always frankly and openly ascribing the sole
praise to God, who doubles, if trusted in with a bold
undoubting confidence, one's natural strength of mind
and body.

The scripture is full of exhortations to "quit ourselves like men,"—"never to faint,"—always to
"rejoice in the hard."

JAN. 27, 1847.

DEAREST MARGARET:—

. . . Young Cuff, the boy so like Walter, is the only
son of a miller near Reading, apprenticed to Blacket,
not 15 yet tho' such a fine-grown fellow. He has very
quiet, unassuming manners. . . . Blacket speaks well
of him. You may or may not wonder, I told Blacket
that when he could occasionally give young C. (who
likes his rod) a summer evening holiday, he might
come and try our water. Told B. the reason; he
is a thoroughly gentlemanly-minded man, understood
it, and thought it natural that I should hear with so
much pleasure that the boy's conduct and prospects
were good; and there is just the sort of look about
him as if he were reasonably happy, but thought
about his mother and his home, which he has not
long left. If all this is foolish, it is my wilful pleasure
to be a fool.

APRIL 20th, 1847.

DEAREST MARGARET:—

It may be well to jot down a sort of journal at odd
times. . . .

After sealing up despatches, a walk with Harry and
Arthur to Newbury—managed with some difficulty to
keep my composure in Blacket's shop; . . . Dropt in
at the Justice's meeting; doggedly went into Blacket's
and talked to the lad on some pretence and came home
much better for it. . . . The appeals from Dorsetshire

are grievous and must be met, and it is difficult to foresee the extent of distress. We must draw our purse strings bravely and pull a strong pull together. . . . Dear Janet has been in such good hands* that I do not worry about her, but it is not that I care about her the less. When she is better we shall have much to talk about. I am sure she will find a corner in her heart and a soothing word at the tip of her pen for one over the seas† who is suffering still more than herself from a common cause. I may be as absurd as the owl as to its own brood, but Nassau, honest fellow, will not laugh at me for what comes to my mind. In Joanna Baillies' "Plays On the Passions," there is a certain personage, the younger sister of the man who commits the murder, the only person whom he seems to love and fear. This personage is, as her friends style her, "The *noble Jane* de Montford." . . . Mrs. Siddons used, in the days of her good looks, to act the part calmly and beautifully. I am metaphysician enough to see how characters tried in one way would act another; and I cannot avoid seeing how the picture is exemplified merely because it has been so under my own nose. Her [Jane's] composure in her own room I shall never forget. . . . I wish I could spare her many a heart ache which she must still expect. These two children were counterparts of each other in most respects and thought and felt together.

Later in the year, impressed more than ever with his wife's character, he wrote to his future daughter-in-law, Fanny, as follows:—

Of my wife, I must need say in honest truth, what you will be ready to confirm, that she is in the select

* Nassau Senior was also at Ventnor at this time.
† Miss Charlotte Shiels.

class of Première qualité letter A, No. 1, of unselfish people, a sort on whom I set a very particular value, independent of any reasons of my own. Altho' that, adding my recent experience to that of several years as a clincher, I never knew any woman in whom strong feeling was so largely combined with unbending moral courage; a quality which all worth their salt, love and respect. . . .

In the same strain he writes to his wife:—

I did not tell you how pleased I felt to read what you said as to the relief of making other folks happy, and that trials did not shut one up. But you always acted on this, and now feel the relief of having made it an habitual thought. . . .

The following was written by John Hughes to his wife while she was still at Ventnor. It refers to a suggestion made by some friends that Jane should have an expensive horse.

. . . Now as to B.'s offer: in any case pray thank him for it. But what think you yourself? Is it really necessary for Jane's health to ride on a high-spirited hunter in Hyde Park? If so the thing is said and done and 50 guineas paid, which I dare say I can manage to find somehow, the other two [horses] would fetch nearly that money, and after the summer I could sell Raven for what sum he would fetch, (mean time I hope you will hire such cavalry as are to be had in Ventnor in case it is good for Jane to ride, as I dare say it may be) but B. differs from me in all his notions of appliances and appearances. He has a right to spend freely, as in good truth he does, a large income gained chiefly by his own honourable exertions; his family is small and will, I dare say, in virtue of their mother's patrimony, be individually as well off as our own people. I having a somewhat large family, whose provision, save some £5 or £6,000, is a trust bequeathed to me by others, am bound to do them all justice. Above all things, I am desirous that their habits should be simple and unpretending, as a source of happiness and independence. Query, therefore, whether it would be well for Jane (because she is a fine girl, who would look well on a fine horse and be noticed by B.'s people,) . . . to be introduced into the equestrian world in a character inconsistent with her future position? She will marry probably on an income very limited for London or suburban wants, and never likely to increase beyond what a family keeping house will require where house rent and taxes and living are high. . . . I am sure that with her excellent sense and conduct, fore-warned will be fore-armed, and that she will be a sheet-anchor of good counsel and honourable thrift to Nassau. . . . Meantime should we be right in putting her, as it were, out of her hereditary ways and habits? and confusing her correct ideas? A cob or two by the sea-side, rough and ready for herself and a brother or so, would be perfectly in keeping and it is not a question of money that I mind. Let us have your own opinion on all this. . . .

This is John Hughes' last word on Jane's education. He had more to say, however, concerning the up-bringing of his boys. He always aimed to have them under the authority of teachers who were honest, straightforward, and manly. Dissatisfied with the young man who had been giving them lessons, he wrote the following trenchant letter to his wife:—

There is always an over familiar air among young women in this "Petit Cherubino de Mozart" that disgusts me often. . . . I believe him a worthy person at bottom, but this does not promise well in some points; there is a foundation of selfishness which is bad. There is the same difference in men as in animals, domesticated. Neptune is shrewd, well-conducted and civilised. So is Jacko. But Nep always is thinking, "what shall I do for the Governor?" Jacko, "what shall I get from the Governor?"

On the same subject he writes to a son:—

I don't wonder you don't like the Cherubino sort; Sharp's antipodes, I opine, Hastings' and yours I am sure, sniffling and snivelling and confidentially earwigging young women to gratify their own conceit; foozling about Tennyson, and women's flounces and mild melodies in the Elijah and the d——l knows what. . . .

If I must have snobs, give me men! I relish not the shabby genteel. . . . A cur is a cur, and so there's an end of the matter.

To his wife he writes as a finale:—

I like very much the way in which you speak of the conduct becoming us in the case of K.; to say nothing of the matter out of our own family . . ., but we are not bound to ignore the difference between a gentleman and a snob, the example is bad for our own boys, if they see a breach of trust not noticed, which I should have been ashamed if any of them had been guilty of. . . . I am sorry it has been a matter of anxiety to you when I meant you to enjoy yourself. You are right, one can never exclude care. . . . Right again as to obedience being the best comfort; go doggedly before your nose and do your duty, which is

partly bearing and forbearing and partly encouraging
right conduct, and discouraging wrong, or else one
walks about with a lie in one's mouth. Right you
are too, as to love and to one's fellow creatures, but
one cannot be wrong in letting degrees of this depend
on their Christian merits.

Later in the year the father took "Janet" to Lady
Salusbury's at Offley, her brother George's future
home. From there he wrote to his wife as follows:—

The place is very pretty and complete; all this
Jane will describe, I dare say, but will of course say
nothing about herself to gratify Mama's conceit.
However, Mama may be perfectly satisfied as to
Miss's tournure and self-possession. The case is much
like a cuckoo's egg in a hedge-sparrow's nest. I
thought I was breeding her up for a quiet little country-girl, and she pops out a natural woman of fashion,
or rather to correct myself, as I am no fashion lover, a
"personage, comme il faut." . . .

This last hint in her father's letter points to the fact
that Jane had changed from a girl to a woman. We
are never taken into her full confidence again. We
have no more diaries to tell us her secrets, and her
letters, open and candid as they are, have little about
herself in them. Moreover, for a period of twenty
odd years, we can give only two short notes in her
own hand, and not a single autobiographical line to
tell us how the joyous, care-free "country-girl" became the gracious hostess of a London house, and the
one of all others to whom her family and friends
turned in joy or in trouble.

and his boy here for Xmas, but he is quite uncertain whether the old Chancellor will indulge him with a holiday at all. . . .

Your most affectionate mother

MARGARET E. HUGHES.

It was during Mrs. Senior's early married life that her musical powers were recognised by her father-in-law. He sent her to Manuel Garcia, one of the most skilled musicians as well as the most famous singing teacher of the day. Garcia was delighted with Mrs. Senior's voice, and put the question to her, whether she wished to have a mere parlour training or whether she wished to study as an artist. With her usual sincerity and thoroughness, she chose the latter course. For two years she worked steadily at dry technique, as if studying a profession, and sang nothing but the scales and exercises her master prescribed for her. At the end of that time she emerged from his hands a finished musician, with the clear and unaffected utterance which had always been hers, combined with the power to bring out the most beautiful tones of her voice without an effort.

After she and her husband had lived in Hans Place for some time,—just how long we do not know,—they went to share the home of old Mr. and Mrs. Senior at Hyde Park Gate. Mr. Senior was a well-known and much esteemed political economist. He had the gift of collecting all the notables of the day about him, and his house was a gathering place for foreigners who, like De Tocqueville, shared his tastes. The

THOMAS HUGHES.

(From a photograph, taken about 1870, by Mrs. Cameron.)

rare charm of his daughter-in-law added a new attraction to his home. Her enthusiasm for pictures and gift for modelling brought artists about her, while music-lovers and musicians came to hear her sing.

Countless as were the friends she made at this time, they did not absorb all her thoughts and energies. She was always, as we have said, the one to whom her brothers and parents turned in time of trouble; and their interests were so identified with hers that we give the family history as being in part her own.

Thomas Hughes had married Miss Frances Ford in the August of 1847, and had gone to live in London. To them were born nine children, of whom seven lived to manhood and womanhood.

He early fell under the spell of the Reverend Frederick Maurice, the preacher of whom men said the same truth shone in his face as fell from his lips. "Tom Hughes," as he was always called, was one of the most lively and active of men, quick to adopt new schemes for benefiting his fellow-man, and eager to carry them out; and the teachings of Maurice had a marked influence upon him. His profession of the law took up much of his time, but "The Working Man's College" and co-operative movements of all kinds claimed his energetic assistance. He was a hearty sympathiser of Cobden's and Bright's and between 1868 and 1874 served as liberal member of Parliament. Yet earnest as was his work, and countless as were his activities, he will ever be best known as the author of "Tom Brown's School Days"—a book he dashed off in his holidays, and intended chiefly as a memorial of his beloved master, Thomas Arnold.

We know that in general Mrs. Senior sympathised with her brother Tom's liberal views and philanthropic schemes; but the only proof we have that this was the case consists in a brief note to Mr. C. E. Maurice, promising to use such influence as she had in securing the nomination of a liberal member of Parliament.

In 1852 George Hughes married Miss Anne Stewart, the niece and adopted daughter of Lady Salusbury, and to them were born four sons, of whom all lived to manhood. George had begun his career as a promising young lawyer; but he gave up good professional prospects, like his grandfather before him, in order that his wife might live in her old home and devote herself to the aunt who had brought her up.

Mrs. Senior was always a welcome inmate of George's house, and a great favourite with his wife and children. She used to sing at his village concerts, and help him whenever her many other occupations permitted. The story of his life is so fully told in "Tom" Hughes' "Memoir of a Brother" that we need give no further details of it here.

John Hughes became a clergyman. In April, 1853, he married Miss Elizabeth Courtney, a clever, amusing, and kind-hearted woman, of whom his family became very fond. She was, however, a number of years older than he. At the time when their engagement came out, Mrs. Senior wrote the following letter to Hastings. The lilies to which it refers were some which he had gone far into the country to gather, knowing them to be her favourite flower.

TUESDAY, June, 1853.

DEAREST HASTINGS,—

You are a darling. I never saw anything so lovely as the lilies, and it was such a very kind and pretty attention of you. My rooms are lovely with them.

I send you Mother's two last letters. I shall try to go to Brighton to spend a day with them next week.

John writes me that he is going to be married to a Miss Elizabeth Courtney, a niece of Lady Catherine Bereas. She is ten years older than he, and an invalid and not rich, but he seems to be very much in love so I have written to *congrat.* him.

Ever dear boy, your affectionate sister

JEANNIE.

Hastings was only twenty at this time, and he looked on his future sister-in-law as superannuated and rapidly nearing the grave. At first he could not be enthusiastic over the match, though he did his best to hide his feelings from his brother. On one occasion, shortly before the wedding, the two had a farewell evening together at John's bachelor quarters. They sat for a long time in silence, the elder rubbing his hands before the fire and looking about him in calm satisfaction. Suddenly he remarked, in slow, contemplative tones, "Well, Hastings, I think on the whole it is a very excellent arrangement"—a sentiment which he would undoubtedly have expressed with equal conviction at any period of his married life. For forty years he led a tranquil existence as Vicar of Longcot, Berkshire, scarcely leaving his parish save to attend an occasional concert in London, and died loved and honoured by his people.

John Hughes, the father, died in 1857. During the days of ill health and depression which preceded his death, he wrote once more to his wife about his daughter Jane. By this time Donnington had been sold, and the move made to Boulton's, London—a change most hurtful to one as dependent as Mr. Hughes on active out-door amusements. He grew ill in the city, and went to Southsea for his health. His wife was detained in London, nursing a case of illness—probably smallpox—among the servants. Mrs. Senior, however, and Henry and Arthur were able to accompany him.

Years before, the letters to his wife had spoken of Jane as a child "needing a mother's care" or, later, as a "personage comme il faut"; now, however, he wrote, "Jane is really everything, God bless her, to me and the rest; there is no end to her cheerful helpfulness." The tables were turned, and he was now as dependent on her as she had been on him.

It is curious to note that one of these letters, of 1857, is the sequel to the one of 1847, in which he spoke of his reasons for not giving Jane an expensive horse. He had then expressed his wish that she might be economical in her habits; now he writes as follows:—

It is a pity there is not a church-society adopting Quaker costume or somewhat like it for conscience sake; and it is a blessing not to live among what are called fashionable people, to whom these extravagances are law; but not to women like Jane, who, among other good qualities, has a conscientious sense, like yourself, of the use of money.

In the last letter of Mr. Hughes' from which we quote, he gives us an inkling that Mrs. Senior was not taking care of him for lack of other occupation.

SOUTHSEA, January 5, 1857.

DEAREST MARGARET,—

... Now to yourself and Jane. She is determined to return here, for which God bless her, tho' I could be well content to try and make it out without her, wanted as she is elsewhere, and I myself certainly improving. I long to have you out of that house of ours in any case. Certainly I never had so distinct an idea of this dreadful pestilence as now. . . .

You want a week's cessation of all cares at Walsham to make you all right and you know you are the sheet anchor of the whole concern here and elsewhere. I need hardly say how much love I have to send you from the two boys.

Ever your affectionate,
J. HUGHES.

On the other half of one of these letters we find the following note from Mrs. Senior herself, which, owing to a slender hinge of paper, was placed with her father's correspondence instead of her own. We give the whole of her letter. The "Nina" mentioned is Mrs. Inglefield, of whose Paris letters we find mention later.

MY DARLING ANGEL,—

Papa offers me room in his envelope and limits me to half a sheet, and to please him I accept, for it would make him really unhappy if I wasted another envelope and Queens Head on you! So I consent to do so for once and must write very small to get as much as I can into my half sheet.

Mammy darling, you would really be happy to see Papa to-day. He is so *very* much better. He had a good night and eat a very hearty breakfast. We went out to drive for an hour and a half, and he would have walked afterwards, only the rain came on. He is quite cheerful to-day and (the best sign possible with him) he has begun *talking* again—Holding forth. —He has been talking about his past life and I have been preaching him a *most admirable* sermon. He speaks much of Mr. Mathias and would I am sure derive great benefit and happiness from talking to him. The text of my sermon was, that all that retrospect of the *past* was wrong, as it unfits a person for doing their duty in the *present*. But it is a great comfort to see Papa so much better—I shall leave him now with perfect comfort, for he is quite in the right way to get all right, please God. I long to see *you* my own darling, and to see you looking better too—Nina and I have been walking. Her babies and Leslie are all darling children. We met Frederic A. who ran to a distance and kept saying, "Touch me not." As if one had any desire to touch him!!!

God bless you, my own,

Very affectionately,

JEANNIE.

When Donnington was sold, the three younger boys were well grown. Hastings, "the mealy-faced boy," was in the sherry trade; Henry, "the beef-faced boy," had finished school; and Arthur, "the squab," had shot up into a fine lad with a military career in view. The three made their sister's house the base of operations for private theatricals and amateur concerts and the starting-point for "larks," such as an evening at the opera, or a good play. Hastings and Henry, who lived in London with their parents, were constantly dropping in to lunch or tea, and Arthur spent as much time there as vacations allowed.

In his boyhood Henry had had a severe illness which had left him almost paralysed. Of course it was his sister who had helped Mrs. Hughes to take him to Brighton for sea air, and who had shared with her the duties of nursing. A famous masseur, called Harrup, had undertaken his cure and literally rubbed the numb limbs back into life. Henry completely recovered, and in after years became an athlete at Cambridge and a crack oar on the river.

Leslie Stephen was his tutor in college. In his essay on "Forgotten Benefactors," written many years later, he cited Henry Hughes as an illustration of how an obscure and far from brilliant or conspicuous character might influence his fellow-men. The writer's estimate of his former pupil is too true and beautiful not to quote.

Long years ago I knew a young man at college; he was so far from being intellectually eminent that he had great difficulty in passing his examinations; he died from the effects of an accident within a very short time after leaving the university, and hardly any one would now remember his name. He had not the smallest impression that there was anything remarkable about himself, and looked up to his teachers and his more brilliant companions with a loyal admiration which would have made him wonder that they should ever take notice of him. And yet I often thought then, and I believe, in looking back, that I thought rightly, that he was of more real use to his contemporaries than any one of the persons to whose influence they would most naturally refer as having affected their development. The secret was a very simple one. Without any special intellectual capacity, he somehow represented with singular completeness a beautiful moral type. He possessed the "simple faith miscalled simplicity," and was so absolutely unselfish, so conspicuously pure in his whole life and conduct, so unsuspicious of evil in others, so sweet and loyal in his nature, that to know him was to have before one's eyes an embodiment of some of the most lovable and really admirable qualities that a human being can possess. . . . [His companions] might affect to ridicule, but it was impossible that even the ridicule should not be of the kindly sort; blended and tempered with something that was more like awe—profound respect, at least, for the beauty of soul that underlay the humble exterior.

During the twenty years following Mrs. Senior's marriage, two of her younger brothers passed out of her life. In 1862 Henry Hughes died from the effects of the accident to which Sir Leslie Stephen refers; five years later, Arthur died in India where he had been sent with his regiment. It so chanced, however, that fate wove ever closer the web which bound her to her brother Hastings.

Anna Duke Clark.   Arthur Octavius Hughes.   William Hastings Hughes.
Jane Elizabeth Senior.   Nassau John Senior.   Emily Adelaide Clark.
Henry Salusbury Hughes.   Mary Clark.
Walter Nassau Senior.

(From daguerreotype, taken at Tenby in 1857.)

In the summer of 1857 Mrs. Senior with her father, husband, and son went to stay at Tenby, where Archdeacon Clark and his wife, Mr. Senior's uncle and aunt, were living with their three daughters. Mrs. Senior had her three younger brothers down for a two-weeks holiday by the sea-side, and the six young people enjoyed themselves mightily, scrambling about among the rocks and caves, hunting for sea treasures, and leading a care-free life, half-in and half-out of the water. We can imagine how Mrs. Senior must have entered into their fun. She even consented to have her picture taken, sitting in their midst. (A reproduction of the daguerreotype is given here.) By the time the two weeks were over, Hastings and Emily Clark had become engaged.

The wedding took place in 1858. Hastings and his young wife spent their short married life partly in Spain, partly in England. They had three sons, William, Gerard, and Henry, and one daughter, Emily, born in Spain in December, 1863. When the baby girl was only ten days old, the mother died suddenly of a fever, and the young husband was left with four children on his hands, alone in a foreign land. No sooner did the news reach England, than Mrs. Senior wrote to him begging him to bring his children to her house, to be mothered and cared for as her own. She told him she longed to comfort him herself, but that "dear mother" had so set her heart on going to "her boy and his bairns" that she felt it wisest to put aside her own wishes in the matter. The warm invitation was accepted with as warm a gratitude, and the three boys and little girl came to live with Mrs. Senior.

One and all the children adored her. She completely won the hearts of the eldest two: Billy, a reserved, independent lad, who in after years gave her name to his only daughter; and "gentle Gerard," who, when only in his teens, copied a full-length portrait of her as a labour of love. Little Harry, known in early days as "the wobbler," would make for her whenever she appeared, with open arms and unsteady legs. When he was a half-grown boy, she wrote of him, "He is too enchanting with his sweetness now I am ill, always coming to see me—Bless him!"

Mrs. Senior had the baby girl's cot placed beside her own bed, and always looked after the child herself when she was ill. The little girl soon learned that, at a word from her, her aunt would rouse instantly, and get out of bed on the coldest night to fetch hot applications for an aching ear, or remedies for a cough. Yet the absolute unselfishness of Mrs. Senior bred a curious spirit of chivalry in the children under her care; and the small girl often bore her own pain in silence rather than disturb her too willing nurse.

Homer never mentioned a man or woman without coupling their names with some epithet which gave the key to their appearance or character. He spoke of the "white-armed Helen," "the discreet Penelope," and many more we could call to mind. If he had sung of Mrs. Senior, we wonder what he would have called her. Would it have been merely "the fair-haired"? Or would he have chosen, as he did for those dear to him, some less superficial name, and called her the "golden-hearted" or the "clear-eyed"?

Mrs. Senior brings to mind an old Celtic legend of the race from which she sprang, that tells of a sister and three little brothers turned into wild swans and condemned to spend three hundred years on the sea of Moyle. The storms came and the spray flew, but she found a rock on which they could light; and through the long winter nights she sheltered one brother under each wing and the third beneath her breast. Time swept two of Mrs. Senior's younger brothers away from her, but left the third, together with his four children, under her wings until the end.

CHAPTER VII.

ELM HOUSE—INMATES AND FREQUENTERS.

We chance to have no accurate knowledge of the
exact date when Mr. Nassau Senior rented "Elm
House." His father died in the spring of 1864, and
the move probably took place about that time. The
house stood on "Lavender Hill," and had several
great English elms in front of it; when the family
moved there it was surrounded by fields, though
during the next ten years the city crept rapidly
around it. It was a large house—as it had need to
be—square and deep, with a garden at the back and
pasture for a couple of cows. Mrs. Senior welcomed
to this home her mother, her brother with his four
children, and, later, her mother-in-law. To the
already large household was added a young girl
whom her father, an Indian officer, left in Mrs. Senior's
charge. Different as were the interests and occupations of these inmates, the convenience and taste of
each were considered. Mr. Senior had his own
smoking-room and library, the two grandmothers their
separate apartments, and the little people were sent
to play where they could not annoy their elders.
What harmonised this heterogeneous family was an
open secret to those who watched Mrs. Senior's sunny
and decisive rule.

JANE ELIZABETH SENIOR.

(First sketch of head for portrait, by Watts.)

Of Elm House and its presiding spirit, Lady Ritchie gives the following description in her short article called "In my Lady's Chamber."

Some of us may still remember Elm House, where the Seniors lived at Wandsworth, and the long, low drawing-room, with its big bow-window opening to a garden full of gay parterres, where lawns ran to the distant boundary, while beyond again lay a far-away horizon. It was not the sea that one saw spreading before one's eyes, but the vast plateau of London, with its drifting vapours and its ripple of housetops flowing to meet the sky-line. The room itself was pleasant, sunny, and well-worn. There were old rugs spread on the stained floors (they were not as yet in fashion as they are now); many pictures were hanging on the walls; a varied gallery, good and indifferent; among the good were one or two of Watts' finest portraits, and I can also remember a Madonna's head with a heavy blue veil, and in juxtaposition a Pompeian sort of ballet girl, almost springing from the frame; and then, besides the pictures, there was a sense of music in the air, and of flowers, and of more flowers. The long piano was piled with music-books. Mrs. Nassau Senior, the mistress of the house, used to play her own chords and accompany herself as she poured out her full heart in strains beautiful and measured rather than profuse.

Garcia had been Mrs. Senior's singing master, and he would sometimes be present among the rest. I heard him speaking of her with affectionate admiration when he was a hundred years old, in his honourable age. How clear was her voice, how it rang and vibrated! For those who loved to listen to it, her "Vado ben spesso" rings on still. The true notes flowed; she did not seem to make any effort. She would cease singing to give some friend welcome, and take to her music again as a matter of course. There was no solemnity in her performance, and yet I have heard Mrs. Sartoris say that it was because of the unremitting work of years, and because of Mrs. Senior's devotion to her art with absolute and conscientious determination, that she could use her voice as she did with tender and brilliant ease. It was a good sword indeed to defend the right. I heard a pretty story of a room full of Whitechapel boys and girls in revolt, and suddenly, when the clamour was at its height, she stood up quietly and began to sing, and the storm stopped and the room became silent and attentive. Sir Theodore Martin told me that he had only met Mrs. Senior once,—one day when she was singing an Irish ballad to George Eliot at North Bank, "Far from the land where her young hero sleeps," which was written of Emmet. Sir Theodore said that forty years after he "could hear the notes still quite plainly." Some voices have this peculiar quality of vibrating on and on.

Lady Ritchie has painted for us pen portraits of Mrs. Senior, but others have done us the same service with the brush. Millais, when painting his picture "The Rescue," chose her for the model of one of the central figures—that of a mother. holding out her arms to receive her child from the hands of a fireman. Apropos of this, he wrote the following letter to Mr. Tom Taylor.

HANOVER TERRACE,
REGENTS PARK.

MY DEAR TAYLOR,—

I am so struck with Mrs. Senior's beauty, that I hope some day she will sit to me. Although I have not the reputation for painting beauty, yet I think I can appreciate it in nature; and I am very anxious to get a beautiful face for what I am painting this year. I hope you will use your influence in my behalf to get her to sit to me.

Ever truly yours,
JOHN EVERETT MILLAIS.

She has such lovely hair, besides face, I am certain I can paint a head from her that all shall admire. Let me know if it is possible.

Later he wrote to Mrs. Senior herself.

MY DEAR MRS. SENIOR,—
I am really very much delighted that you like the picture. I was afraid that you were disappointed, and did not like to write about the exhibition, from your silence after the private view. The loaf was delicious. Unless you go out of town very shortly I hope to see you before I leave.
I believe that the "Rescue" will be engraved; if so, you shall have your likeness, as I will remember to send you an engraving.

Yours very truly,
JOHN EVERETT MILLAIS.

We see that Mrs. Senior must have been favouring the artist with a sample of home baking. All Mrs. Hughes' apprentices made wonderful bread—light and with a crisp golden-brown crust—and no doubt she or her daughter had had the training of the Elm House cook.

Another portrait of Mrs. Senior, now in possession

of her son, was painted by Watts. The painting itself is best described in the artist's own words, in the following letter to Mrs. Senior.

I shall of course take pleasure in doing anything that may improve the likeness, that I fear can never be very satisfactory; you must be my eyes. To-morrow I want a long day for the drapery that worries me. On Friday, if you will bring the drawing, I shall also be ready for a sitting. . . . Thanks for the glass and lace, I think both will do. I send you the box, &c. and I sincerely hope it may be the means of supplying you with some amusement and a new and very safe object of interest. It is not a very grand present, but I hope it will remind you of my picture, and the meaning I have in making you water (in the picture) a flowering root with so much solicitude! As I told you, I intend by the flowers to typify the better sentiments, aspirations, and affections which it is sometimes difficult to keep alive, or at least blooming in the crush of artificial society. But I love to think of you as cultivating these beautiful and rare flowers! no, not rare; . . .

> By God's dear grace not rare,
> In many a lonely homestead blooming strong
> Mid haunts of men requiring watchful care
> Where in tumultuous rush the passions throng
> Lest haply they, the fostering hand not nigh,
> Withered by breath should fade, too rudely brushed should die.

There! that's doing a bit of Phillips! mocking the Muses. But if you laugh at my poetry, you won't at my intention. . . .

Your most affectionate friend,
THE SIGNOR.

JANE ELIZABETH SENIOR.

(Portrait by Watts, taken between 1865 and 1870.)

As may
o Millai
ir own
aled h
ad well.
s a stri
iefore h
Mrs. Sei
the bene
Senior v
i woul
part, hc
ier and
Thou
Senior s
be tern
scores
their t
standir
the fol
were
label
friend
in qu
first e

It
"We
perso
to sa
can't

As may be seen from her gift of a home-made loaf to Millais, Mrs. Senior's household extended beyond her own walls. Watts was among what might be called her greater family,—those whose comfort and well-being she had now and then in charge. It is a striking instance of his reliance on her, that, before he married Miss Ellen Terry, he besought Mrs. Senior to take her under her roof, and give her the benefit of her motherly care and insight. Mrs. Senior was too wise to consent—with her household it would have been impossible. This refusal on her part, however, never altered the friendship between her and the artist.

Though Miss Ellen Terry was never included in Mrs. Senior's greater family,—what in hospital phrase would be termed her "out-patient department,"—there were scores of young girls who were. Many poured out their troubles in her ears and found her an understanding listener. From her letters to one of these, the following passages must have been taken. They were found among some old papers and bore the label "Extracts from Mrs. Senior's letters to a young friend." They were evidently written when the girl in question was having some home difficulties. The first extract is as follows:—

It is all very well in you to say "Don't judge," "We can't judge," but that is not the point. If a person commits a murder or steals, it is not judging to say, "'A' murdered 'B'" or "'C' has stolen." One can't shut one's eyes to certain facts, and it would be only affectation to say, "Oh no, I don't know if 'A' murdered 'B'; tho' it is proved in a court of justice; to say so would be judging." I don't judge them in my sense of judging. I mean, that tho' their conduct appears to me quite unjustifiable and cruel, I don't condemn them, I feel sure they have blinded themselves. . . .

I tell you I can't understand them in the least. How you can live in a state of perpetual restraint among them all is marvellous. . . . How can any of you consider that to be like loving each other, for sympathy and openness and tender thought for each other's sorrow is the foundation of family love. The one strain of your letter is, "what is the good of being truthful, they can't understand, so I will hold my tongue." Would they not understand at last and alter, if you were more frank and spoke up? . . .

I don't think we ought to let people do wrong, if by protesting we can make them see the light; though I understand the temptation of "letting things be." I don't think it a bad thing "to owe it to one's self" (in the best sense,—everything can be twisted and corrupted) but it is a form of "Noblesse oblige" that means, "However disagreeable, I will not do what makes me despise myself, I owe it to myself to be able to respect myself,"—that is my idea of "owing it to one's self." I quite grant the phrase is often perverted so as to mean, not what one owes to one's self as the "Temple of the Holy Spirit," which temple we are trying to keep fitly pure, but what do we owe to what others may think of one's self, or—what do we owe to our own pride, conceit, and so-called dignity.

The second extract goes on:—

If a quiet life, dear, were the first thing to desire for one's self and those we love, I should perhaps agree with you in what you say of ——, that "we ought not to wonder that *her* strongest feeling is to give her husband his way and spare him pain. While we are upholding that the love of husband and wife is the master feeling, she carries it even further than we do, that is all." It is just because we are to leave father and mother and cleave to husband and wife that we are bound, I think, to be *faithful above all things* to our husbands and wives. If we see that our "partner" is doing wrong or selfishly, I think our duty is to remonstrate lovingly and firmly; if we give our partner his way to spare him pain, we are unfaithful to a sacred trust.

We are not called on to criticise those whose lives are slightly bound up with ours (indeed we never need criticise any one or speak hard and painful truths), but to the people to whom God has related us very intimately I think we are bound to be utterly truthful and faithful, and, if needs be, not to shrink from paining them and ourselves by pointing out where they seem to us wrong. The bond of husband and wife is quite falsified if it does not imply openness for mutual improvement.

I am full of faults and am painfully conscious of them, and I like a quiet life, and I hate to find fault with others, particularly those I live with, but I think I could be faithful and tell Nassau if I saw him exercising authority over Walter to do something that Walter objected to do and which he was bound to do by no real duty. . . .

The last of these extracts refers evidently to Bacon's famous Essay:—

As to truth and Bacon, dear, I am not able to judge. I started life with no moral courage and with the belief that love was better than truth; and I own that I have come to think that absolute truth, the most open and unvarnished truth, is the noblest, happiest thing in the world. All virtues and beauties and joys seem to me to hang on it, and certainly I can't love a person and be in communication with him without putting truth before all things. If one has "hidden corners" it destroys all the comfort of love for me. But I don't say you are wrong to say a word on the other side; there is much to be said on all sides. But for myself, I could not have confidence in my dear ones without absolute openness. Because they see my faults and I see theirs, the love is not less, and if one says "I don't understand this in you. That does not seem clear to me," the love grows by the absolute confidence that comes from such explanation. Indeed I could never absolutely love and trust a dear one unless I could say and hear all without hurting and being hurt. But no two people are just alike, and some people can't love without mental reservations even with their dearest, I believe. I recognise it, and God knows I don't condemn it. But I don't sympathise with it.

Mrs. Senior's gift for singing, together with her generous use of it, led to friendships in the musical and philanthropic worlds,—friendships with men and women of earnest purpose, long experience, and tried capacity. She became by degrees a co-worker with them in the struggles taking place under the surface of life in the great city. One of these friends was Jenny Lind Goldschmidt, and we give here three of her letters to Mrs. Senior.

OAK LEA,
WIMBLEDON PARK,
S.W.
SUNDAY EVENING.

DEAR MRS. SENIOR,

Indeed it will be with greatest pleasure to make some "rendez-vous" with you now and then, in order that we may bring our voices into harmony. For with your talented nature, and really artistical singing, it will be a treat to me seldom before experienced to listen to you and sing with you.

Yours very sincerely,
JENNY LIND GOLDSCHMIDT.

OAK LEA,
WIMBLEDON PARK,
S.W.
23 Nov.

DEAR MRS. SENIOR,—

More than thanks for your charming, genuine letter; you are a born artist, that is what you are. I often think of you that I should like to know you are earning two thousand a year by giving singing lessons in London. You are the very person a lady is wanting. I would give you some hints, tell you anything I know about singing; and why should you not, in the prime still of life and strength, do a work which would be both honourable, profitable to yourself, and a benefit to many. Do think about it. I think "Ruth" was one of the few fine performances I have heard during my long career; certainly the choruses sang admirably, and everybody showed such kindness that we cannot be grateful enough. "Ruth" must be heard and known often before one can really judge of the value of the music.

I would indeed be delighted to sing "They that sow in tears" with you; can you not get it up for the eighth, when I trust you and Mr. Senior will dine with us.   Do try, whenever you like to come to me and let me come to you.   I owe you a visit, we could then sing together and I could tell you a few things I wish you to know about teaching.

God bless you.

Yours affectionately,
JENNY LIND GOLDSCHMIDT.

Mrs. Senior followed the advice given in the above letter and gave singing lessons for a time in London.*

OAK LEA,
WIMBLEDON PARK,
S.W.
Wednesday.

DEAR MRS. SENIOR,—

You are dear, and good; it is sweet of you to sing with me.   Our little matinée is to be on the 15th of June, I think, as that seems the only day on which Mr. Hallé can help us; but you will surely sing a solo, one of the fine English ballads such as "Barbara Allen" and others.   Well, I shall come and coax you.

Yours affectionately,
JENNY LIND GOLDSCHMIDT.

The above letters are undated, and therefore have been given here to show the kind of friendships she formed between 1848 and 1868.   The following letter concludes this period of unrecorded years.

* In a letter to Mr. Forbes, February, 1872, Mrs. Senior wrote, "I am proud to say I make some very tidy earnings with giving singing lessons, and I am *immensely* proud that I can contribute to the family purse."

OFFICE OF WORKS,
WHITEHALL PLACE,
LONDON.
Jan. 5, 1869.

MY DEAR MRS. SENIOR,—

You were carried by the "angel ever bright and
fair" before I could thank you, last night, for your
great kindness in coming amongst my Southwark
friends, and express my delight at your exquisite performance of the music which you had so judiciously
chosen. I am sure you will believe that I was grateful to you. As regards the audience, you will, I think,
have felt that you never sang before one which more
thoroughly enjoyed your singing, and more eagerly
desired to show their appreciation of it in the only
way they could do it. I only wish that you had been
present to hear the enthusiastic response which they
gave to the thanks offered to you in their name by
Mr. Newman Hall and myself. You scarcely know
the good you do by coming amongst these poor people,
and humanising and elevating them by such pure and
simple enjoyment as they derived from your singing.
The good you have done is the only return which I
fear you can expect for the trouble you so kindly took
yesterday. I wish that there were more like you in
the world, we should be much better for it.

Ever yours sincerely,
A. H. LAYARD.

By the time this letter was written, Mrs. Senior
was already acquainted with Octavia and Florence
Hill, "George Eliot," Florence Nightingale, Sir
Charles Trevelyan, and many others, and the next few
years brought her shoulder to shoulder with them in
the ranks of the practical reformers.

CHAPTER VIII.

LETTERS—1870–1872.

On July 19, 1870, the Franco-Prussian war broke out. The following letter, however, from "George Eliot" betrays no suspicion of the coming storm. She wrote it in March, just before setting out on a trip to the Continent.

From M. E. Lewes to Mrs. Senior.

THE PRIORY,
21 NORTH BANK,
Mar. 13, 1870.

DEAR FRIEND,—

Bless you first of all for being a good woman, and next for being good to me. The Sachet came to me quite safely, smelling like the garden of Eden in its most desirable spots where the violets grew. So you will be hovering about me like an invisible angel with violet scented wings. Very delicate scents make me feel happy, but I find it too troublesome to get them for myself, so such a present as this is really a greater addition to my pleasure than it would be to most people's.

Keep a little love for me till we come back, for I shall think of you as one of my friends who make an English home dear, and enter into my life quite out of proportion to the number of times that I see them. One lives by faith in human goodness, the only guarantee that there can be any other sort of goodness in the universe. See how diffusive your one little life may

be; I say that apropos of your longing for a wider
existence. Pray offer our kind regards to Mr. Senior
and think of me often as

Yours always affectionately,

M. E. LEWES.

The next three letters are from Mrs. Senior to her
son, written after the outbreak of the war.

Mrs. Senior to W. Senior.

27 AUGUST. LAVENDER HILL, LONDON.

. . . Poor old Monsieur dined here, more miserable
than I can describe. He has offered his services to
the Head of the Hospital service; but as he is an
Orleanist, it is quite possible that his offer may be
refused. The suffering from want of comforts and at-
tendance is awful. Strong men are needed, the work
is too hard for women. But if I were free, I should
go, for I know I can nurse well.

I think every strong young fellow who is capable of
self-sacrifice, and is in earnest about his life, ought to
offer to go and help. I would go to-morrow if I were
a free man.

The misery and suffering haunts me day and night.
I have had a letter from Mrs. Inglefield; they are
turning Versailles into a great hospital; lots of families taking in wounded. She asks me for help; I
had already sent all the money I thought I had a
right to spend, to the International Society; but I
have been looking out all that I can spare of my linen,
&c., and have just come back from leaving it at the
Depot, with a quantity of provisions fit for the sick,
which I got at the Civil Service Stores. Mrs. Inglefield says that famine is imminent, and provisions not
to be bought in Paris; not a ham, or a bit of salt meat

could she get. Oh! dear, dear, what a time! And in
Alsace and Lorraine the peasants are starving. I shall
send off a lot more things next week. I must help if
I sell the clothes off my back. It is of no good to try
to enjoy anything. I really can't. The spectre of
the state of things in Germany and France comes
between me and all pleasure; and I am ashamed of
my ease and luxury in the presence of this war.

J. E. S.

Same to Same.

10 SEPTEMBER, 1870, LAVENDER HILL, LONDON.

. . . You will see by the papers that the Republican
Government profess that they won't cede an inch of
territory; though they wish to make peace. It is
certainly very hard on the Republicans, that they,
who were the only members of the Corps Legislatif
who protested against the declaration of war, should
find themselves called on to prosecute it now. If
only the Germans would treat for peace, and ask for
nothing but the payment by the French of the expenses of the war, what a noble example they would
be setting to the world. But I fear this is too good
to hope for. . . .

J. E. S.

Same to Same.

3 NOVEMBER, 1870. LAVENDER HILL, LONDON.

I quite think that the King of Prussia is in earnest
in what he said, and says about God, or as he calls
God, "Providence," an expression I especially hate.
I don't think the old fellow a hypocrite, but I hate
his pious telegrams, because he might have made, and
ought to have made, peace at Sedan. Till then I
understood his thanking God for his success, for he
was fighting to defend his fatherland, and to put
down a tyrant who was ruining a noble people. But

now his telegrams make me sick, because, if he chose, he could have peace, and I can't see, when he is sacrificing life on all sides, that he ought to be so sure that God is approving him. For I don't think God can approve of his conduct. Still I don't think him a hypocrite. He has been brought up to think that God likes fighting, I suppose!

J. E. S.

The following notes from Florence Nightingale refer to Mrs. Inglefield's Versailles letters, which Mrs. Senior had let her see.

35 SOUTH STREET,
PARK LANE,
W.
Dec. 29, 1870.

MY DEAR MADAM,—

I cannot thank you enough for sending me these most interesting and invaluable letters. All the information that I receive, even from Germans, goes to bear out exactly what is herein said—tho' said by *your* correspondent with very much more point and piquancy, as you may suppose, than by most of *mine.*

I believe her to be absolutely right in all her "guesses." Might I suggest to you that when the time comes to draw up some conclusions, whether for publication or not, as to the working of different International (Red Cross) Societies with a view of future progress, suggestions quite invaluable will be found in these letters? I have laid many in store, tho' quite deep in my breast.

I am so very sorry about her distress as to the French poverty at Versailles. Mr. Bullock, the gentleman who was the author of what is called the "Daily News Fund," and has been working it himself in the Ardennes, is now gone to Versailles with a similar purpose, I take for granted at your instigation.

You know also of the "War Victim's Fund," (I enclose one of their papers)—86 Houndsditch. E.

Pray excuse a very hasty note, and pray believe me,
Dear Madam,
Yours devotedly,
FLORENCE NIGHTINGALE.

Same to Same.

35 SOUTH STREET,
PARK LANE,
W.
Dec. 31, 1870.

Returned this beautiful and spirited and mournful letter, with very many thanks.

It seems a mockery to wish her and you a happy New Year, tho' I do with all my soul and thought. At least it is a relief that this terrible and dreary and bloody and wicked Old Year is over, laden with the sorrow and agony of millions, which, alas! are not over. People tell me to be thankful that we are "not in it," and so I am, most deeply thankful that our Country is "not in it," but that I am not in it is the bitterest regret of my life. My whole heart and soul are longing to be with those wretched sufferers of the Loire.

I am very sorry that you have an anxiety about "A child." I trust it is nothing serious.
In haste,
Yours overflowingly,
FLORENCE NIGHTINGALE.

Now come two more letters from Mrs. Senior to her son. Though the first says nothing of the condition of France, we give it here because it belongs to this time. The second again treats of the condition of Europe, and is the last we have on the subject.

Mrs. Senior to W. Senior.

27 NOVEMBER, 1870. LAVENDER HILL, LONDON.

... I went to the Workhouse, and was parson to my old women. Then Octavia Hill came, and the Masons; and Octavia stayed on with me till nine. Dear mother is far from well; ... I am unhappy about her. One day she seems better, and then the next she is quite poorly again. Octavia was very interesting, telling me all about the work she is doing in Marylebone, to try to get the people from depending on charity, rather than on their own exertions.* In the court that she manages, she has a workroom, and there the people are given employment, and never money or help without an equivalent in labour of some kind. The clergy are helping her much, refusing to give charity to the people there, so that they may all go to the workroom. Of course there is a great deal of opposition to Octavia, and of ill feeling about it. But she is a splendid and brave woman, and she will live it down, and people will at last see that it was better to help themselves than to live on charity. She says that (as usual) the women are much narrower-minded than the men. The men sometimes own that Octavia is right, but they never dare say so before their wives! and there was a dreadful meeting the other night, when every one seemed against Octavia and she was hissed and hooted, and at one moment she thought they were going to attack her. She is a brave woman. The thing that pained her most was that people should seem so incapable of seeing the truth; and many, of whom she expected better things, said that 3d. given, was better than 5d. earned.

J. E. S.

*See Octavia Hill's Report.

Same to Same.

27 MAY, 1871. LAVENDER HILL, LONDON.

I did not write to you last night. I was reading to Mammy till she went to bed, and then wanted to finish the *Pall Mall*. How dreadful it all is at Paris. Bad though the Communists are, I cannot but feel that they have been made worse by Thiers' insane conduct. It is quite impossible to say how sad it makes me. It is not the awful loss of life, nor the burning of the beautiful things that have rejoiced so many to look at. What really agonises one, is to reflect on the hatred between men and women of the same blood and tongue; a hatred that one fears cannot but exist for many long and sad years. And I see the death blow to liberty too; for every one will be afraid of liberal principles, and republicanism; and political life in France will again be at a stand-still. And the only salvation of France lies in her entering political life as a nation. I think the Versailles people are as bad as the Reds, worse indeed, for they ought to know better. I don't feel the heart to enjoy anything, it is so sad. And it is impossible not to be unhappy about our own country, too. So many will be unable to see the difference between honest Liberalism, and Red frenzy, and will forsake the ranks of true liberality. I know many already who are forsaking their liberal principles, because they cannot separate the truth from exaggeration. It needs great moral courage and strong faith to stand by one's flag, when people say, "you see where your principles lead." Even dear old Monsieur A. calls me a Communist, and says it is dreadful to think that a person whom he respects and values, can say a word for the villainous perpetrators of such atrocities. It is of very little use to try to explain one's views, because he hardly listens;

but the fact seems to be as plain as possible. It is just as unfair and foolish to condemn Christianity for the sorrows of the Inquisition and of religious persecutions, as it is to condemn liberal principles because the Communists have been wicked and mad, and have ended by burning Paris. It certainly is not liberality that leads to these excesses. As for our own country, I think we are in a very sad way. Pauperism growing one way, and the greatest luxury the other; and I think we shall never come to our senses till some awful national calamity overtakes us, and makes us more humble and truthful, and less self indulgent. I can't help longing to be out of it all, and in some nice primitive country, where one could lead a simple life, amongst simple people, in fresh air; where there was food enough for every man and woman who would work. I suppose I am dismal to-day because of Paris, and of spending yesterday afternoon at the workhouse. Every time I am there, I am more and more convinced that something is very wrong in England. Amongst the poor old women I see, certainly eight out of ten are women who have children in service or about in the world. When I think how maid servants and men servants dress, and how extravagant many of the working classes are, I feel that it is an awful thing that they should leave their mothers to go to the Workhouse in their helpless old age, rather than provide for them out of their wages.

Every one is so horribly fond of ease; myself, quite as much as any one. I detect it in others, because I feel it in myself. I am often growling in my own heart at having no carriage, and some other things which would be pleasant to me. But I don't think I should like ease and fine clothes better than helping my mother. At least, I hope not! I dare say the faults of other classes arise very much from the sins of our class. I readily admit that. But the sad fact remains, and it seems such a hopeless business to get anything the least straighter in this stuffy old country that one sighs in a very cowardly .way for a colony. The person who is like a stream of sweet water after wandering in the wilderness, is Octavia Hill. She cheers me more than I can say. She really does something, and that makes her hope, and hope gives her more power to work. I feel a miserable old stick-in-the-mud, sad and hopeless, except when with her, or for a little time after seeing her.

J. E. S.

Mrs. Senior's wish for a wider field of work had led her to offer her services to Miss Hill. From the "Life" of the latter * we quote the following passage: "Miss Hill's friendship with Mrs. Nassau Senior . . . was increased by the ability she brought to bear in the arrangement of the accounts of the houses." These houses were some of the poverty-stricken tenements which Miss Hill had bought for Ruskin in order to get control of the inmates, and gradually to introduce a better standard among them. Unfortunately we have no account of Mrs. Senior's experiences in this work.

The next two letters, which conclude this brief chapter, were written shortly after the sudden death of Mrs. Senior's oldest brother, George. One is from Thomas Hughes to his brother Hastings, the other from "George Eliot" to Mrs. Senior.

* Page 188.

GEORGE HUGHES.

(From portrait by Watts, taken about 1870.)

CRYSTAL PALACE, S.E.
May 24, 1872.

DEAR BROTHER,—

I haven't had heart to write to you before. There has been a lot of business to do, and then I felt how much more bitter the loss must be to you than to any of the rest of us, when you are away in a foreign country with no soul who knew him about you. However, now I am better and have seen a letter of yours which makes me ashamed of giving way to any vain regrets. So I must employ my first spare half hour in writing you a few lines. I was down at Offley only three weeks before the end, went out hunting with him and two boys and never saw him stronger or more cheery. . . . I got down about forty-eight hours before the end and I needn't tell you that he died as he had lived, a model of a brave Christian man. We have lost four such dear brothers and may say with the old Duke of Ormond, we wouldn't exchange our dead brothers for all the living brothers in Christendom. But we must take care of ourselves now, and at any rate run no risks while dear old mother is alive. I am at work on a memoir of him for the boys and though cruelly hard to do, I think it does me good and certainly interests Mother and Annie and Jeanie. . . .

Ever, dear Hastings, your most affectionate,

THOS. HUGHES.

"ELVERSLEY,"
RED HILL,
July 1, 1872.

MY DEAR FRIEND,—

. . . .

You are paying a part of the great price for the blessing of being able to love those near to you. It is of no use to offer words under such a trial. Comfort will gradually come in your activity for others, which never leaves you long in the power of your own particular lot. Some day I shall ask you to tell me all about your family, I mean the family of Hughes, for I don't half know what I should like to about it.

With best regards to Mr. Senior,

Always, dear friend, yours affectionately,

M. E. LEWES.

WILLIAM HASTINGS HUGHES.

(From a photograph, taken in 1871.)

CHAPTER IX.

"NEW GROUND."

While Mrs. Senior was singing for poor folk, helping Miss Hill with the accounts of her houses, or packing gifts for the war sufferers, and while a hundred other vital interests were crowding her life, she was devoting daily and hourly thought to the children under her care. She and her brother Hastings discussed together the various points of their education, among others their religious training. Neither he nor she felt they could honestly teach them exactly as they themselves had been taught. Their talks on the subject resulted in her putting a few of her childish experiences into a paper called "New Ground," which she and her brother intended to amplify. Neither ever carried the idea any further, but we give the fragment she wrote just as it stands.

SOCIAL.

We had a housemaid,—one Sara. I believe she was rather cracked, but she was a kind creature, devoted to sentiment and novels. Scott's novels were always disappearing, the edition I mean in which we children were allowed to revel. We knew if a volume was missing that it would be found in Sara's possession. One day we wanted the last volume of "Kenilworth." Sara was nowhere to be found; at last we routed her out of the closet where dirty clothes were kept for the wash. She appeared with very red eyes, and the missing volume of "Kenilworth" sure enough, and she informed us that she had not gone down to tea because she could not help stopping to read the end of that poor sweet "Emmie Roberts."

She was very humble and cringing in her manner, which used particularly to irritate me, for we children had always been accustomed to associating with old family servants, true friends, with whom we felt on terms of perfect ease and equality, and to have Sara courtesying to me in the passages if she met me worried me and made me shy. One day I met her carrying a lot of brushes, &c., and as she made way for me to go by, a lot of them tumbled, and I picked them up and said "I'm going to carry them for you, Sara, what room?" "Oh! lor! Missy, for goodness' sake put them down, you a young lady to help a poor servant like me!"

Now my father had been reading at family prayers parts of the New Testament which I had inwardly digested and thoroughly accepted; and the outcome was that I said to Sara, "If you are a servant, I am one too." "Missy, you must not say such naughty, improper things," said poor Sara, "what would Missis say if she heard you?" and she tried to take her brooms, but I said, "Well, I *am* a servant and I *will* carry your brooms," and so I did. But poor Sara really was scandali·ed to the heart, for she complained to our old nurse, Franklin, who told me that I "must not say such odd things as I had to Sara because other people might presume on it some day."

So, being snubbed thus, I thought I *had* done something improper, and consequently did not like to ask Mother whether the New Testament was right or whether Sara and old Franklin were right. But I worked out the problem little by little in my own mind, all the more surely for the temporary failure in establishing Christian equality; greatly aided therein by the friendships we had with our old servants and by the courteous, friendly kindness which my father and mother ever showed to their dependents.

RELIGIOUS.

We did not get much dogma taught us by our parents, but we had the usual things taught us by governesses and spiritual pastors and masters. Tho' my father was the most kind hearted and liberal man personally, yet we should never have dared to speak to him of any religious doubts which might trouble us, for he, and my mother also, thought scepticism on religious matters wrong. So we listened to what we were taught and floundered about as we could, among the questions which were constantly presenting themselves for solution.

It certainly is curious in looking back to see how early religious doubts began, and to note the phases one passed through quite unknown to those one most loved.

A very old friend of my father's, Mr. P., had resigned his living because he could not read the Athanasian Creed conscientiously. We were the dearest friends with his children and his wife was an intimate friend of Mother's. We heard him spoken of as if labouring under some awful disease, or as people nowadays would speak of a friend who was possessed by the insanity of drink; as if he was fearfully and grievously to blame for *allowing himself* to have religious doubts, and his wife and children to be intensely pitied for his wickedness in disbelieving the dogmas taught by the church. In the days of which I speak, scepticism, which was generally styled

"Atheism" even by well educated persons, was considered a far more unpardonable sin than immorality.

I think it was soon after we went to live at Donnington when I was about seven and a half years old, that I began to doubt the justice of certain things I had been taught. Especially I could not stand the idea of Hell. I used to teach a class at the village school on Sunday morning, where the tiny children lisped Watts' hymns under my inspection.

"There is a dreadful Hell."

When my brothers were home for the holidays, I used to have neither time nor inclination for dwelling on such matters, but when the vacations were over I used to wander a great deal alone in the fields and lanes and watermeadows, and get much exercised in my mind over theological matters.

A poor girl in the village was dying of consumption; my mother used to go constantly to read to her, and sometimes I went with her, and sometimes alone. My mother used to tell me what a good girl she had always been, and to call my attention to her uncomplaining patience. When I went to see her alone she used to get me to read to her, and generally asked for the 14th and following chapters of St. John's gospel. Several times she spoke of her unworthiness and of her doubts of salvation, and when I said, "But you are so patient and good, and God must love you and make you happy," she used to talk of the blood of the Saviour, and of her fear that she did not trust as she ought in his mediation, and of her own unworthiness, *deserving* eternal flames, unless she could trust in her Saviour's blood. I used, after seeing her, to have fits of exasperation against God, and say to myself, "God's a devil, God's a devil—if He is really what they say. If Anne does not trust in the Saviour, yet she has always been a good girl, and God *ought* to make her happy and if He sends her to Hell, He is very wicked and unjust, and if He is Almighty why should He send any one to Hell? He could make us good if He is all powerful, and if I were able to make every one in the world happy and well I would do so. Even the wicked people I would like to see happy; if they were happy perhaps they'd be good, and if *I* would not have any one unhappy even on earth, I must be kinder than God, for God makes people sick and poor and unhappy on earth and then He sends them to Hell for ever and ever and ever afterwards. So it seems to me that God is a wicked devil."

I remember being alone at the end of a long field when there was an eclipse of the sun, which made a lurid light over the trees and grass and the birds did not understand it, nor did I, and I felt very much awed and thought of the last day (as I had been taught to expect it). And I asked myself if God would, at the last day, damn me eternally because I was constantly giving way to the great sin (as I had been taught) of doubt. I took refuge in the cowhouse with a brindled cow who had just had a little calf, and I remember kissing their noses, and wondering if there could be a future for animals and whether they also would be divided into "sheep and goats" and some sent to Heaven and some to Hell, and then the gloom of the eclipse passed off and I took heart, and determined that I should *not* be a goat at the Last Day.

A beloved old nurse, who had brought us all up, had made the deepest, most painful impression on me one Good Friday, all the deeper because of the awful mysteriousness of what she said. I had some bit of work on hand for my doll, and being intensely interested

in it I began one Good Friday morning to sew at it.
Old Franklin came in and found me in the nursery
busy with my needle and thread. "Oh! Missy,
Missy dear, put away your work to-day," said she.
"Why should I not sew to-day, Franklin?" asked I,
"it is not Sunday." "Oh, Missy, don't you know that
every time that you stick your needle into your work
on a Good Friday it goes right into the Saviour's
heart and hurts him, and brings out a drop of blood?"
I was truly awe-struck. I could not even ask why, or
how, and for years I could not get over the impression
that it caused a physical pain to the Lord if a stitch
was stuck on the day of commemoration of his death.
But I never dared to ask for an explanation lest I
should be guilty of "Atheism."

When I was a little older I had a governess who was
very kind, but peculiarly irritating to me because of her
erratic ways and her genius. Every morning we
read the lessons and psalms for the day. At first I
used to ask bold questions on points which troubled
me, but she was a thorough, ardent Church woman
at that time (tho' afterwards she became an Irvingite)
and did not encourage anything like religious doubt.
I recognised that I must not speak of my *wicked*
doubts to her, so I kept them to stumble over by
myself, and only imparted to her points which were
obscure, but which I had the instinct to know would
not be considered as wicked doubts. I remember
once exercising her much over Melchisedec.

After this introduction, Mrs. Senior goes on briefly
to state her creed.

The essence then of my belief (and all religious
teachers agree, so far as I know, in telling us that
human beings ought to have a belief) is that the

Author of the Universe is a Being to whom we ought
to look up to as an average boy looks up to his father
only with very much more reverence. The average
boy cannot in the least see why, when he arrives at
a certain time of life, his father sends him from all
the comforts and kindliness and grace of home, to
school, a place where he has to lead a rough, unlovely
life, where the boy who sits next him takes from him
his sister's photograph, and very likely the matron
retains, without asking, the jam which comes in his
home hampers. The father knows, from his own
recollection of school life, that all this is likely to
happen, but he knows also that if he keeps the lad at
home much more mischief may be done him, that he
would very probably grow up a misconducted, lawless
prig, or an emasculated creature incapable of understanding and dealing with his own sex. So he sends
him to school, and if the boy turns out badly, if he is
lazy and dirty, and dishonest, does the father, if he is
worthy of the name, cut him off from himself, shut
the door of hope in his face? Does he, however far
wrong his son may go then or in after life, ever permit
the wish to enter his mind that his son should suffer
indefinitely for his bad conduct? Does he not rather
take blame to himself for not having helped that son
to overcome in himself the tendencies to certain
forms of selfishness which he (the immediate cause
of his being) has handed down to him? And if that
father is profoundly convinced that he is a supernatural
being and requires his son to believe this, and his son,
after due reflection, tells him that he cannot accept
this, that he believes him to be of the same nature
as a gorilla only with more intelligence and self-
restraint, does the father, for this, cut off from himself
the son for all this life? And if not, how does the case
stand with regard to our religious teachers? They

tell us to believe in an Almighty Being, the Author of all things, who has put us here in a world of trial, who has given us our reason to use honestly and carefully, and to whom we are to look up as to our Father who is in Heaven. And they tell us that if we fail in doing our duty by our neighbours, but still more surely if we cannot believe in His having done certain things which they tell us He has done, He will torment us inconceivably for ever and ever. And they say, "God's ways are not our ways." And we shudder and hang our heads, till there comes a time when we can stand it no longer and we stand up and say to our religious teachers: "Then so much the worse for the God of whom you tell us. We do believe, in spite of your damnation, in spite of all meanness and misery we see in ourselves and our fellow-men and women, in a Heavenly Father, but we cannot believe that He is less loving to His children than we are to ours.

The following letter from Miss Hill was probably written at about the same time as the above. It indicates that Mrs. Senior must have expressed to her also some wish for "New Ground." Unfortunately we have not got the letter to which this is a reply.

> 14, NOTTINGHAM PLACE, W.,
> December 15th, 1872.

To MRS. NASSAU SENIOR.

As to the points on which you and I equally differ from so many clergymen and churchmen, if we think Maurice's interpretation of the creeds the true and simple one, is it not doubly incumbent upon us to uphold it *in* the Church? Leaving it would be like saying we could not honestly stay in it. Then does not all the best, most thorough, most convincing, most peaceful reform of any body come from within? . . .

Don't think I am special-pleading. Except for the sake of the Church, I don't care where you are. While you are what you are, you are safe everywhere; for you will find grace and goodness in all things; and God's Church certainly comprehends those not in the Church of England. If you are sure that the services do not speak to and with you in words that help; if there is a lurking sense of want of courage or candour in remaining, which is real, not fancied; if you have a sense of antagonism and alienation, not support and fellowship, why not leave the Church? Those who love and know you would never feel you further from them; and, if you found support and peace greater from other teaching and other services, why not go where you would have it? . . .

From these more or less remote thoughts on "New Ground," we turn to nearer and more every-day ones, and to Mrs. Senior's daily care of the children. Her insight into their small pleasures and needs is exemplified in the following letters to her niece, Emily. The first of these was written when the little girl was away on a visit; the last, after the great break in the Elm House circle had been made, and Mrs. Hughes, Emmy, and Gerard had gone to live at the Isle of Wight.

JUNE 7, 1873.

DARLING EMMY,—

It is, I think, your turn for the weekly letter. I do not know if you will have had a letter from dear Granny, so I am sure you will be glad to hear that she got safely to Walsham. She found old Uncle

Tom quite well and waiting for her at the station and she was not very tired. . . .

I had a nice letter from Gerardy. He has learned to ride a bicycle, and so has Walter Simpson, and they seem to think it fine fun. I am going to beg Gerardy to be cautious, for I am always so afraid of an accident. The thing is likely to fall with the rider and break his leg.

I have sent Gerard the paint-box I promised him and three paint brushes and a block of sheets of drawing paper. I call that his measles present, as Harry's measles present was the fishing rod and basket. I think I must give you a leg present for the itching you had on your leg. What would you like, I wonder?

I sent Willie a big hamper the other day, to feast with his friends on his birthday. I think boys at school enjoy that more than anything. . . . I hope, darling, that you practice regularly and steadily. It will be such a disappointment to me if you forget your music as you did last time. Give my love to every one and a kiss to Harry. God bless you, dear little one.

Ever your loving
AUNT JEANIE.

ELM HOUSE,
31st July, 1874.

MY DEAR LITTLE GIRL,—

You must write at once to your Aunt Annita and to one of your brothers. I want you, darling, to be more regular in writing to your brothers and to your relatives. It is a very important duty, for if people love you it gives them infinite pleasure to get your letters and you should not neglect so obvious a duty. . . .

Ever your affectionate,
AUNT JEANIE.

DECEMBER 28, 1874.

DEAREST EMMY,—

This is to wish you many happy returns of your birthday. I pray that each return may find you loving and serving God better than the last. . . .

I send you an envelope for writing to your father. I sent him Harry's letter on Xmas day, but I want you and Will and Gerardy write in this envelope, to wish him a happy New Year. Write as soon as possible. I put thin paper inside, that you may not make the letter over-weight. Oh, how I should like to be at Colwell with you all.

My best love to the dear lads and Bessie and Dyer * and all the rest.

Ever your loving,
AUNT JEANIE.

After their move to the Isle of Wight, the children were not so much under their aunt's immediate care; but even when absent from her she was the guiding spirit of their lives.

* Many years later, in a clearing in the forests of Tennessee, Mr. Dyer still might have been seen presiding over Mrs. Hughes' garden. One day her son Hastings said to him, "Well, Dyer, when your daughter marries and leaves you, I suppose you will go too."

The old man shook his head emphatically. "Not so long as Mrs. Hughes lives," he answered. "I gave my word to Mrs. Senior that I would never leave her"—a promise he loyally kept.

CHAPTER X.

MRS. SENIOR'S LETTERS TO "THE TIMES"—HER APPOINTMENT.

"Will you send me a copy of the papers respecting 'Boarding Out'? I should like to send them to Mrs. Nassau Senior," wrote Miss Octavia Hill to her sister in May, 1869. This gives us a date before which Mrs. Senior was probably not an authority on the boarding-out of pauper children, and after which her study of the system began. Three and a half years later, in the autumn of 1872, her first articles on the subject appeared. A battle royal was raging at the time between the defenders of the institutional education and the promoters of the home training of waifs and strays. To understand the bitterness of the controversy, we must realise how hard most of the chaplains and directors of London pauper schools had been working for the reformation and improvement of their system. They had separated the pauper children from the adult members of the workhouse, and placed them in "District" and "Separate" Schools; but here their imagination stopped, and it was with unqualified dismay that they saw the wave of reform which threatened to inundate the structures they had so elaborately reared. Defenders of the old system and promoters of the new all wrote voluminous letters to *The Times*, which, as usual, gave place in its columns alike to explosions of wrath and long-winded arguments.

The controversy was started by an attack in the *Clapham Observer* on the North Surrey District Schools, which was quoted in *The Times* of August 16. Various school authorities made the accusations the subject of vehement denial and acrid rejoinder, while the promoters of "boarding-out" seized on them as valuable data for proving their case. Mrs. Senior took her stand in the discussion by the side of Miss Catlin, Miss Florence Hill, and Sir Charles Trevelyan. We give here extracts from four of her letters to *The Times*. What the opposing arguments were, we may gather from her own writings, and from two extracts which we quote from letters written on the other side.

AUGUST 27, 1872.

MRS. SENIOR
TO THE EDITOR OF "THE TIMES,"

Sir,—During a twelve years' experience in this parish I have had much experience among the poor, and can answer for there being no exaggeration as to the state of the North Surrey District Schools. I can speak not only of the physical, but also of the moral deterioration of the children coming from these schools. In several cases I have found in them a positive inability to see the difference between right and wrong, and a general dullness and apathy which has not been overcome for years after their return to family life.

. . . .

I remain, Sir, your most obedient servant,

JANE E. SENIOR.

SEPTEMBER 30, 1872.

MRS. SENIOR

TO THE EDITOR OF "THE TIMES,"

Sir: The advocates of the boarding out system realise as fully as does Mr. Bartley himself that there are two distinct classes of pauper children:—1. Orphans and deserted children, who remain permanently at school; 2. Children of casual paupers, who occasionally leave the district schools to join their parents when the parents leave the workhouse for absences more or less long.

In his letter to *The Times* of 24th of September Mr. Bartley speaks of harm done to children of the 2nd class, who on their return disseminate in the school physical and moral disease contracted during their residence among the "very dregs of society."

I think that Mr. Bartley, if consistent, ought to side with, rather than oppose, the advocates of boarding-out, whose views, if adopted, must necessarily cause an entire separation between the two classes of children, the casual pauper children alone remaining in district schools. . . .

The advocates of boarding-out are quite ready to grant that the plan is "beset with many dangers." But no change would ever be effected if possible dangers were allowed to hinder needful reforms. . . .

I remain, Sir, your most obedient servant,

JANE E. SENIOR.

LAVENDER-HILL, WANDSWORTH-ROAD.

Here follows the letter on the other side.

OCTOBER 2, 1872.

MR. SIKES,

TO THE EDITOR OF "THE TIMES."

Sir,—Theoretical and sensational statements relating to the North Surrey District Schools and to the

boarding-out system have now surely had their run
and it is high time to appeal to facts. . . .

Mrs. Senior lately said that in several cases she had
found in them [those who had left the schools] a positive inability to see the difference between right and
wrong. This is a serious statement, and one which
should not be made without due consideration of
facts. I have been lately appointed chaplain to these
schools, and may, therefore, consider myself free from
all personal motives in writing this letter. I feel,
however, that I should be doing an injustice to the
late chaplain and to all those who have laboured for
years and are still labouring here, did I not contradict
the statement now so freely circulated that the children from these schools turn out badly—I appeal to
facts, and by facts I am willing to stand or fall. I
have the late chaplain's report for last year now
before me, in which he says:—

"Looking at the moral results, I think we should
thankfully acknowledge the success of our labours in
the returns I present to you. I have only found one
bad child among 138; and in this I do not reckon the
unreported ones, four of whom I have reason to believe
are doing well. The single exception to our encouraging list is the case of a boy who ran away from his
place with a sovereign which he was sent to change.
Not one girl, as far as I know or can ascertain, is leading a vicious life, and it is most pleasing to report
that our girls generally are almost invariably found
possessed of modesty and self-respect. Of those who
had left previously I have found two—one boy and
one girl—who must be classed as bad, giving as the
result of the year's inquiries 3 bad children to 269
doing well or fairly. *Allowing for the difficulty of positive knowledge*,* I do not think that the vicious children
are more than 4 per cent."

* Italics ours.

Here Mr. Sikes goes on to ask, first, whether there
are homes enough to accommodate all the children;
second, whether the influence of such homes would
be as good as that of the schools; and, third, whether
the boarded-out children would be guarded from
their bad relations. He answers all these questions
in the negative and then proceeds to his fourth and
most crushing argument, as follows:—

Can the boarding-out system provide so that many
children shall not eventually be massed together in
one family, or district? This massing together, according to the advocates of the system, is our great
evil; and yet, according to Sir Charles Trevelyan's
letter this morning, a lady in Surrey has 12, while a
clergyman and his wife in Buckinghamshire have 16
placed out among his parishioners (how many in one
family not stated). Doubtless this massing would
increase under the boarding-out system, and in time
we should have in effect a number of private boarding-out schools subject to no official inspection save
that of some clergyman or lady visitor, whose interest
would vary from time to time. Here, on the other
hand, we have constant inspection, and, although
Miss Florence Hill is convinced, after anxious inquiry,
that the data do not exist from which any reliable
information can be drawn whether the children turn
out badly or not, I would inform her that it is my
duty as chaplain (and I believe it is the duty of other
chaplains) to visit the children regularly, and to enter
their characters in books kept for that purpose. These
books are open to her inspection, and although I am
ready to admit with her that a *large number do pass
out of sight** (I will not admit that they are forgotten),

*Italics ours.

yet surely under the boarding-out system a time must come when the children will pass out of sight, and be no longer tied to the apron strings of their foster parents. . . .

I remain, Sir, your obedient servant,

JOHN CHURCHILL SIKES,
Chaplain of the North Surrey District Schools.

OCTOBER 5, 1872.

MR. VIGNOLES
TO THE EDITOR OF "THE TIMES."

Sir,—As my official connection with the above schools has been several times referred to in your columns, I ask for a very limited space to add a word or two of my own to confirm in every particular the admirable letter of my successor, which appeared in your impression of Wednesday. . . . My duties here are too close and continuous to allow me to enter at any length into the controversy, so I must content myself with simply stating that the boarding-out system in or near London would be a complete failure; and I have very great doubts of its success anywhere. The real difficulty in dealing with pauper children is the interference and bad influence of friends and relatives. . . .

I am, Sir, your obedient servant,

OLINTHUS J. VIGNOLES.

OCTOBER 9, 1872.

MRS. SENIOR
TO THE EDITOR OF "THE TIMES."

Sir,—Mr. Sikes asserts that the statements relating to the North Surrey Schools, made by the advocates of boarding-out are "theoretical and sensational, and rest on visionary foundations."

The facts to which these "sensational statements"

allude were officially published, and were made the object of a Report of the Local Government Board; they are, therefore, not likely to be incorrect. Contagious disorders were represented as prevailing in the school, and the children were reported to have been out of health and underfed. Mr. Vignoles (late Chaplain of the School) asserts that the children are well fed; but this was not the opinion of the Guardians who drew up the report, and the following quotation from the *Clapham Observer* of the 28th of September shows that ill health is not decreasing in the School:—

"Mr. Hanson . . . said that the returns that day showed that the number of sick children had increased from 96 to 380."

Both Mr. Vignoles and Mr. Sikes, the present chaplain, speak very positively of the moral success in life of the children who leave the Annerly schools; but Mr. Sikes admits that "a large number pass out of sight."

What becomes of the girls who "pass out of sight?"

This is a point to which advocates of boarding-out would especially beg attention. A girl of 16 is sent from a District School to a situation. She is probably unhandy; the mistress expects too much, and perhaps is cross and impatient. The girl runs away, or "passes out of sight." She has no home to go to, and no one would be made unhappy by her misconduct. It is well known by those who have studied the subject that many of these girls go on the streets.

Under the boarding-out system the girl would have a strong incentive to resist temptation in the knowledge that any misconduct would cause pain to the one who had taken charge of her. The lady who had undertaken to look after her during the period of her boarding-out would not lose sight of the girl, and masters and mistresses would probably be more forbearing if they knew the child was not friendless. In case of leaving her situation, the girl would have a temporary home with her foster-parents, and a friend to help her in the lady who had superintended her education for many years.

Even with the best and kindest intentions on the part of the officials, it is not possible that each child among several hundreds brought up together should have individual training. Rules must be observed, and the officials have no power to set them aside, even if they would. About two years ago a lady living near the Annerly schools applied to the master for leave to take 250 children to the Crystal Palace. The master was most kind and courteous, but was obliged to refuse her request, as all amusements outside the walls of the institution were strictly forbidden. She then asked to be allowed to visit the sick children in the infirmary, to tell and read them stories and give them toys. This, also, the master was obliged, most unwillingly, to refuse, the Board having decided that, as the children would have to lead a hard life when they left school, they should have as few pleasures as possible while they remained there; that no influence from without should be brought to bear on them; and that they must look to the institution alone for food, mental, spiritual and bodily.

No chaplain, master, nor mistress, however conscientious and hard-working, can educate and influence 600 children at once. It is inevitable that most of the children brought up in these large schools should be turned out, as Sir Charles Trevelyan truly says, listless and apparently half-idiotic. What other result would be expected from such a joyless, monotonous training?

Your obedient servant,
JANE E. SENIOR.

LAVENDER-HILL, WANDSWORTH-ROAD.

OCTOBER 22, 1872.

MRS. SENIOR

TO THE EDITOR OF "THE TIMES."

Sir,—I have been waiting some time to see if any new difficulties in the way of boarding-out should be brought forward by its opponents. Apparently all that can be, has been alleged against it and may be summarised in the four following objections:—

1. That sufficient number of suitable homes could not be found. To this objection the experience of one county alone is ample answer. At a meeting held in Birmingham in 1869, a letter upon this subject from Sir William Johnstone was read, in which he says:—"I was authorised to send circulars to the established and dissenting ministers, and to the medical men of every parish in the County, requiring to be furnished with the names, addresses and characters of such persons within their boundary, as might be safely entrusted with the board and care-taking of one or more children, and at what rate per week. The replies to these circulars were so numerous and so satisfactory that although from 300 to 400 children had to be placed out, no fewer than 130 applicants were disappointed in receiving boarders after the whole had been provided for."

I am certain that anyone who has lived in the country will bear out my assertion that in every parish at least two or three families would be found fitted for the trust and thankful to undertake it.

2. That proper supervision would be wanting.

The supervision would be ample, and from various quarters,—viz., the Boarding-Out Committee, who settle preliminary questions, and to whom appeals are made; the clergyman of the parish (or the Dissenting minister if the child is not a member of the Church of England); the master or mistress of the school which the boarded-out child would be compelled to attend; the inspector, who would make his visits at unexpected times; and above all the lady or ladies who undertake to be responsible for each child, who look after and visit it frequently and report regularly to the committee.

3. That the boarded-out child might be unkindly treated by the foster-family.

The character of people applying to receive the boarded-out child would be strictly investigated by the Boarding-Out Committee before a child was intrusted to their care; while the constant and unexpected visits of the lady who undertook to be answerable for the wellbeing of the child would make any ill-treatment impossible.

4. That the relations of the children would get at them, and might exercise an evil influence over them.

This difficulty is especially referred to by Mr. Sikes in his letter of 9th of October. In placing children belonging to London and suburbs in country homes, nothing would be easier than to send them to parishes where they had no relations, and the plan adopted at Birmingham would of course be followed. There the Poor-law officials are strictly forbidden to give to anyone the addresses of children boarded-out. When deemed advisable the committee themselves communicate this information to any well-conducted relations of the child.

The undeniable advantages offered by the boarding-out system over education in large district schools are these:—

1. The orphans and deserted children when boarded-out are entirely separate from the children of the casual paupers.

2. The evils in a sanitary point of view, of bringing

up children by hundreds together are avoided. Why should children be denied the physical advantages bestowed on young foxhounds? Masters of hounds have learnt by experience that puppies get shaky on the legs and die of distemper if brought up in large numbers together at the Kennel, so the pups are sent out "to walk" at neighbouring farmhouses.

3. The cost per child in boarding-out is less than at district schools. The weekly cost at the Liverpool District School in 1869 was 5s. 3d. per head; at Manchester, 5s. 7d.; at Leeds, 7s. 7d.; at Edinburgh where the system has been at work for 30 years, the number of children boarded-out in 1868 was 349 and the cost of each child came to exactly 3s. 6d. a week, including every expense. . . .

Mr. Sikes demands proof that a large proportion of pauper girls go on the streets. The experience of Mrs. Way, Miss Florence Hill, Miss Turning, Sir Charles Trevelyan and others who have gone thoroughly into this subject, shows that this statement is not lightly made. A year or two ago a Board made investigations into the conduct of their girls after leaving their care. ⅕ did very well, ⅕ pretty well, ⅕ indifferently, ⅕ badly, and ⅕ (that is one in every five) was on the streets.

Mr. Sikes is hard on the "ladies who spend their time in advocating the boarding-out system," and "thinks we should be better employed in establishing and supervising industrial and other homes where children might go on leaving schools of service." It is just because we are all closely connected with small individual homes that we desire to deliver children from the stupefying influences of large district schools, and to place them in the healthier atmosphere of country homes. For, in watching the workings of these small industrial schools we have learnt to ap-

preciate the great benefit of individual training and
of an approximation to home life and influence.

I am your obedient servant,

JANE E. SENIOR.

The Times gives Mrs. Senior the last word and then
puts on its judicial spectacles. In a leading article
of October 24, it sums up the evidence in an impartial way, and then, with a sudden turn which must
have surprised and exasperated some of its readers,
it sides with the advocates of "Boarding-Out." "A
number of well informed persons," it says, "assure us
that the requisite foster-homes are easily to be found,
and that we may forthwith emancipate pauper children
from an unnatural life. . . . It would be folly to refuse
such an opportunity without a trial." . . . "We are
content to admit that experience must decide whether
their plans are practicable; but we must also say
that it would be very short-sighted and ungenerous
to refuse to allow the experience to be gathered. The
authorities of District Schools, instead of arguing
against 'Boarding-Out,' would act more worthily in
showing some gratitude for a proffered co-operation;
and the spirit displayed in the course of the controversy
has certainly reflected more credit on the innovators
than on their opponents."

At the time of the above controversy, Mr. James
Stansfeld, the Director of the Local Government
Board, was looking for some woman to undertake the
inspection of the pauper schools for girls in London,
and to criticise them from a woman's point of view.

Knowing Miss Octavia Hill's capacity for putting her
hand on the right person for any work, he asked
her whom she could recommend. She at once suggested Mrs. Senior, and brought about an introduction
between the two. Miss Hill wrote the following letters
to Mrs. Senior at this period.

NOVEMBER 18th, 1872.

I had written to Stansfeld before your letter arrived,
but have only just received his reply. I want you to
meet him before we enter upon the question of your
fitness in any detail. I have therefore told him
nothing but that I think I know some one who will
do. He is coming to the party of the 28th, as he has
long wanted to come to one; and I shall introduce
you to one another there, if all be well. I am sure
that you are the very person; and if he has any sense,
he will feel this. We shall see. . . .

CROCKHAM HILL FARM, EDENBRIDGE, KENT,
January 3rd, 1873.

DEAREST JANEY,

Stansfeld wrote to tell me that he had written to you.
Oh! I do long to hear the result. If you cannot do it,
no one can; and it wants doing, so I hope you will try.

I am so thankful and so touched about your help
about the Public-house. You are the only person
except myself who has as yet found a soul to help. I
can't tell you what a sharing of burdens it feels. I
am nearly sick of writing about it, or rather of the
thought that by any post now the matter may have
to be decided; and I may not know of enough money
to say, "Let the arrangement be made." I dare not
promise a farthing more than I have been promised.
I never trust to the future for help; it would seem

to me wrong, as I have not of my own what would
enable me to meet the engagement; and, tho' one
must get something more, one never knows how
much. . . .

I do not know when I have felt such joy as on receipt of Stansfeld's letter; oh! Janey, do try the work
if you have a chance.

I am ever your loving friend,

OCTAVIA HILL.

Same to Same.

JANUARY 5th, 1873.

Thank you most heartily; your offer of help did me
more good than anything; somehow such a spirit
puts new heart into one. I had a very nice letter
from Stansfeld, telling me result of the interview; he
appears to be highly satisfied. God bless and help
you in the work. I am a little sorry in one way that
it does not take you more away from home. I hoped
that you might have had a few hours to rebound from
the weight, and might have been stronger for home
work for the daily absence. But, in some ways, it will
make the work easier; and I suppose the sense of
progress and of public work do one good any way,
and carry one thro' a great many small and some
most heavy trials with a sustaining sense that there
are larger and deeper interests than are contained in
our own circle, which is so small, tho' so dear. So
the work may help you thus after all, as I'm sure you
will help it.

You don't fancy for a moment that I would be so
mean as to take your money. No, Janey dear, I
could not. Spend it nobly and well as you are sure
to do, but don't think of giving it to me. We will try
yet, in trust that there are richer people enough forth-
coming to do the thing. . . .

As may be gathered from the foregoing letters, Stansfeld was satisfied that he had found the right woman to fill the post. Fortunately he was not alarmed by the outcry which had been produced by Mrs. Senior's letters. He was no more afraid to stand under fire than she, and he eagerly welcomed so stanch a coadjutor.

In January, 1873, Mrs. Senior was made inspector of schools—temporary inspector, by her own wish; for being the first woman to fill such a post, she preferred to have her appointment regarded as experimental. She foresaw that her position might be rendered far from easy by the irritation she had caused certain of the school authorities in the preceding controversy, and by the opposition any further criticism from her would be likely to arouse. To be sure, the Local Government Board had approved of giving "Boarding-Out" a fair trial; but it was not with the Local Government Board that she would have to deal. Conservatism in any department of government is hard to battle with, and this made Mr. Stansfeld's loyal support the more helpful and inspiriting.

With the following letters of congratulation from Mrs. Lewes ("George Eliot") and Florence Nightingale, we conclude this chapter.

THE PRIORY,
21 NORTH BANK,
REGENTS PARK,
Jan. 24, 1873.

DEAR FRIEND:—

We had already been told something, though inaccurately, of the good news before your letter came, and we had felt it as a New Year's gift to us. Our joy is without misgiving.

We feel sure that your good work will be done well, and may all blessings attend you in it, over and above the affectionate wishes of your friend—wishes which you will carry with you like a host of encouraging guardian spirits.

The influence of one woman's life on the lot of other women is getting greater and greater, with the quickening spread of all influences. One likes to think, though, that two thousand years ago Euripides made Iphigeneia count it a reason for facing her sacrifice bravely that she might help to save Greek women (from a wrong like Helen's) in the time to come.

There is no knife at your throat happily; you have only got to be a good faithful woman such as you have always been, and then the very thought of you will help to mend things. Take it as a sign of that, when I tell you that you have entered into my more cheerful beliefs and made them stronger because of the glimpses I have had of your character and life. I don't wonder at your not being able to come just now, but you know that we are always glad when you can manage to get to us.

Yours with sincere affection,
M. E. LEWES.

From Miss Nightingale.

35 SOUTH STREET,
PARK LANE,
W.
Jan. 28, 1873.

MY DEAR MADAM,—

I rejoice more than I can say that you have this work to do. You are the person to do it, and no one else. And I would most gladly serve as your hand-maid in it if I could.

. . . .

As I need not say to you, it would be the most conceited thing in the world, if it were not the one I am most disinclined to, for me to give you hints.

You who have done so much for the Boarding-Out in Families, the greatest step of all in favour of these poor girls who are to be our future mothers.

I would think it a privilege to see you if I thought I could be of the slightest use. But besides that I do not think so, I am at this moment engaged, not exactly in a similar inquiry, but in seeing all the Nurses and Matrons in training of our Nurse Training Schools every day. I am pretty nearly worn out, not having got a third through the whole. But, if any point arises in which you think I could be of the slightest use, please command me. Write to me first what it is, and then command my best consideration and answer, either by word of mouth or letter.

I give you joy, or rather I give Mr. Stansfeld and the girls joy. Good speed.

Ever yours most truly,
FLORENCE NIGHTINGALE.

JANE ELIZABETH SENIOR.

(From a photograph, taken by Mrs. Cameron about 1874.)

CHAPTER XI.

WORK AS INSPECTOR (1873–74)—LETTERS.

The full tide of work and service culminated for Mrs. Senior in the months between January, 1873, and December, 1874. During that time—a period of almost two years—she held the office of School Inspector. At first the appointment was, as we have said, only temporary. After a year, it was made permanent. The experiment had succeeded.

Unfortunately, hand in hand with Mrs. Senior's new and great opportunity for usefulness came her illness. At first she had hopes of a quick recovery, and she laid aside the active part of her work during the winter of 1873–74, thinking she might continue it indefinitely later. She took it up again in the spring of 1874, after her reappointment; but, before the end of the year, it became only too apparent that she had no longer the strength for it. She could barely struggle on till she completed her report for the Local Government Board. Then she resigned.

During her two years of service as School Inspector, Mrs. Senior not only investigated conditions in London, but carried her researches into Scotland and France. During her voyages of discovery she made many friends. One, Sir Arthur Mitchell of Edinburgh, used to speak warmly, in later years, of her thoroughness and method. We have no account, however, of the people whom she met, nor description of her experiences.   Neither have we anything to show us how, in her London work, she gathered that devoted corps of helpers, with whose co-operation she traced the careers of the pauper girls.   What we know of her work we must gather from her own impersonal account of it in her report.

In the following letter from Mr. Stansfeld, we get the first hint that Mrs. Senior had already in mind that idea of a central home for girls which later was realised in the Metropolitan Association for the Befriending of Young Servants.

LOCAL GOVERNMENT BOARD,
WHITEHALL,
March 31, 1873.

DEAR MRS. SENIOR,—

I am very glad to hear of your intended visit to the Lakes and Scotland to see the children who are boarded only.   Could you not now, or at some future time, also visit and compare your impressions with those recorded by Mr. Davy, Mr. Doyle's assistant, in the paper I showed you some time ago?

Whenever you are ready to discuss the subject of the possible separation of the permanent from the casual pauper children, I shall not only be ready but glad.

Indeed to speak frankly, I wish you would not be so very economical of my time.   I take an interest in your work, and should like to see its progress in your own thoughts.   It is most natural and best, I cannot but think, that we should talk *frequently* about it; and so far from such discussions being a tax upon my time, they will be a great pleasure and a real relief, because they will mean a sympathetic study of what is most interesting and most needing original and sympathetic investigation in our system.

Do you think of the "Central home" for girls as an official or voluntary institution?

Your statement that the orphans (I don't know whether you would add the "deserted children,") are physically better than the casuals is quite new to me, and is very important, if true.

I hope you will specially notice whether the sleeping wards at Annerly are close and unwholesome, because of the want of ventilating arrangements or because the people won't use them.

I can hardly tell you how thoroughly I think and feel with you, when you say that the more you see and think of the whole subject the sadder it seems, and deeper and deeper still the evil seems to lie. . . .

Truly yours,
J. STANSFELD.

The following letter from Mrs. Lewes, written six months later than the above, voices the growing anxiety of Mrs. Senior's friends on the subject of her health.

BLACKBROOK, BICKLEY, KENT.
September 23, 1873.

DEAR FRIEND,—

.   .   .   .

Mr. Lewes had urged me to write after hearing from Mr. Hughes that your health had been suffering from the strain of work, but I was not sure that a letter seeming to ask for news would not be less friendly than silence. Hardly any one in our choice list of beloved Sisters has been oftener spoken of between us than you, and I feel as if I had something good this morning now that I have had a letter from you.

O dear, I can only groan over your bodily afflictions.

It is no use to wish it had befallen an idle woman, or, in general, to allow oneself wishes about what cannot be altered. . . .
Your faithfully affectionate,
M. E. LEWES.

We wish that we could give the paper which called forth the following very explicit letter from Mr. Stansfeld. It must have had some electricity in it. Mrs. Senior had received many shocks in the course of her investigation, and was ready to use her pen, ink, and paper as a conductor by which to transmit them to sleepy officials. The only result, in some cases, seems to have been a half-awakened growl from those who did not like to have their slumbers disturbed.

LOCAL GOVERNMENT BOARD,
WHITEHALL.
November 19, 1873.

DEAR MRS. SENIOR,—

This *will* do and *well*, you have only to go on. It is all very well to call yourself a quaker and to say you feel such, but I do not think you very quakerish or "peace at any pricey," when you got on the subject of one of the secretaries of the Local Government Board, and I think I know who would come rapidly worse off in a duel in that quarter.

But do not misunderstand me, I don't ask you to be antagonistic, or narrow, or anything but what you are, just generous and sympathetic, but bear stiffly in mind (this is all I have to say) the nature of the business which you have undertaken, and of your own responsibility to it as a woman, in your own judgment solely of that responsibility.
Yours very truly,
J. STANSFELD.

We must now turn from Mrs. Senior's work to her stay at the Isle of Wight. We may gain a fairly clear idea of it from the following description by Lady Ritchie taken from "In My Lady's Chamber":—

. . . There is a letter with a date to it, February, 1874, written by Mrs. Senior from a little cottage in the Isle of Wight, which Mrs. Cameron had lately altered and devised, and which has belonged to the writer at intervals for years. That one winter Mrs. Senior went there to stay in it. Her son has let me see the letter, which begins with a motherly blessing, and then continues: . . .
"What a grace is rest to those who work without ceasing!"
There is a description of an evening at Farringford and of the mysterious walk there—the great veiled stars and the dark garden with its great shrubs and the great room and the poet within, reading, and Lady Tennyson, like St. Monica, lying on her couch. All this was but a short break in the constant unending work of Jeanie Senior's life, in her gallant fight with suffering. During the first week of the holiday she could not forget, she could not rest, but after her three weeks she writes to her son: "I feel perfectly up to my work now, and have fits of longing to be at *Paupers* again, though in general I am absorbed by the delight of the beauty of everything, and the desire to pass the remaining years of my life in painting scenes in the Isle of Wight! . . ."
She described a visit she paid with Mr. Watts to a cottage her mother, Mrs. Hughes, eventually bought:
"The garden was most sunny and warm, and the view of the heath and the sea really lovely. There was a high north wind, and the colour of the sea,

light green and purple, with splendid white tops to
the waves.   The bit of heath, too, is lovely, but there
is no field for a cow, which would be a drawback in
mother's eyes."

Some other painter should have been there to paint
the two figures looking across the gorse common at
the white crests of the waves.   Watts with his serene
and stately looks, the lady, who had but such a little
while to live, but who to the last tried for practical
beauty in life as far as in her lay, and happiness and
deliverance from evil for others.   And among all her
good practical works the Metropolitan Association
for Befriending Young Servants has been one to last
and to spread its useful harvest under the care of those
who have come after her.   "Mabys" perhaps sprang
from the foam of those waves that day as they broke
upon Colwell Bay.

We give in full the letter to which Lady Ritchie
refers, from Mrs. Senior to her son:—

FRESHWATER, ISLE OF WIGHT,
March 8, 1874,
BEFORE BREAKFAST.

We had a never-to-be-forgotten evening on Friday
at Tennyson's.   The most poetical evening I ever
remember in my life.   We walked up at 8, in a very
still, dark evening, only the big stars showed at all;
and then they were veiled in vapour, as if shining
through tarlatan.   Then Farringford is as quiet as
a tomb, when you get inside the grounds, and the
house is sheltered by big shrubs, which in the mysterious darkness looked enormous.   Mrs. Tennyson is
a very remarkable looking woman; I suppose she is
not, and never has been really goodlooking.   But
she is beautiful, a paradox you will have sense to
understand.   She looks like a saint; and I thought

of St. Monica, Augustine's mother, all the time I looked at her. She is a great invalid, and looks thin and worn; but placid, with the sweetest voice, and a gracious, gentle manner. She had on a grey dress, and a great deal of soft white lace and frilling about her, and a soft white burnous, fastened on each shoulder. Altogether a most charming sort of vision. We talked a little to her, and then Tennyson came in, and soon began to read to us. You know how much I like "Maud," and how little I agree with those who think it inferior to his other works. I thought I knew it well, but as he read it, a thousand new beauties appeared, and I felt that I had never half appreciated it. He is evidently much distressed, annoyed would perhaps be the right word, that the work has been so coarsely and unintelligently criticised. And as he went on, he told us the silly criticisms that had been made. Mrs. Tennyson showed by her remarks that she disapproved of his letting himself be stung by these absurd criticisms. He told us that he believes he is the first poet who has written a drama, told throughout by one character; and then he repeated over and over again how unfair it was to say it was a disjointed work; for there never was a story more connected, which is perfectly true. The mad bit he wrote off in twenty minutes. He said that Forbes Winslow, the Doctor for madness, had told him that it was the only description of real madness since Shakespeare, because it is a picture of a mind overthrown. Madness, as represented by many, is not madness but drivelling. Tennyson reads in a sort of low chant, with a curious fall of voice at the end of a phrase (sometimes the phrases are very long), a fall of a musical sixth, I think. You cannot imagine how it moves one. All theatrical element is banished, yet it stirs one to the depths; perhaps the quiet and solemnity, and the absence of all sensationalism is what *does* move one so. I could not help dropping some tears, which I thought no one saw! Had I begun to say anything in the way of thanks, I should have begun to howl and sob, which would not have been pleasant for them or me! We got ourselves off as soon as the reading was over. One thing that I felt all the evening was how I wanted you to enjoy it with me. We got outside the house, and found the evening quite clear, the stars like diamonds, and the moon reflected in the sea. Tennyson directed us how to go a shorter way back through his shrubberies into the lane; and finding our way through the dark, unknown shrubberies was exciting. The night was lovely. I don't know why there is something "eerie" in the moon when it is waning, but so it is, though it was very beautiful.

J. E. S.

We have one more letter from Mr. Stansfeld written before the publication of Mrs. Senior's report. It refers to the promise given by Mrs. Senior and her co-workers, namely, not to reveal the names of those mistresses who had given information concerning the servants they had taken from pauper schools.

STOKE LODGE,
HYDE PARK GATE, W.,
March 25, 1874.

DEAR MRS. SENIOR,—

It is quite clear, I think, that you cannot comply with T.'s request; you must not break your word to those whom you promised that their names should not appear, nor should the information they gave you be put in such a form as to implicate them. You must adhere to this promise strictly whatever happens.

But independently of this, Mr. T.'s request is, in my mind, objectionable and quite inadmissible in its present form. His observations have been invited, whereupon he writes to you as if he had been invited to test the accuracy of your statements of facts, which was quite another thing; and indeed as if his function now were to sit in judgment upon your conclusions also.

You must not allow this. He would not address a male inspector in the same way; it is your right and your *duty* to hold your own as an equal. I am leaving town to-morrow morning until after Easter or else I would come and see you for I do not feel able to advise in detail, especially as to what information you may safely and fittingly give Mr. T., without a talk or reference to the statistics which he impugns. I would specially under the circumstances, suggest that you should make a friend of L. and ask his advice, he is such a real gentleman and of so impartial a mind; indeed you *must* now make friends, for there may be a set at you and it may not be perfectly easy to stand alone. . . .

If you hold your own, but patiently and prudently, I think all will probably come right. They cannot, if they wished, go to extremes, and "abolish" you without my making it a parliamentary question, and that they will not willingly do. I would suggest your seeing L. and B. before answering T., possibly they may advise your asking him to call on you that you may show him what you can.

Truly yours,
J. STANSFELD.

A governmental Blue Book is four inches thick, and broad and long in proportion. The Encyclopædia Britannica is light reading compared to it. The particular one entitled "The Third Annual Report of the Local Government Board, 1873–74," which was "Presented to both Houses of Parliament by Command of Her Majesty," contains eight reports on Pauper Schools, written by two doctors and six inspectors, and addressed to Mr. James Stansfeld. One of these inspectors was Mrs. Nassau Senior. Although one of her co-inspectors questioned whether the poor-law guardians ever read what he had to say, and although Mrs. Senior's report covered eighty-four closely written pages, we doubt if any member of "the boards" omitted to read it. It was too well advertised—by its opponents.

In order to collect the data on which to base her report, Mrs. Senior went through all the Metropolitan schools with care and thoroughness—such thoroughness that she even pounced down on one at 5.30 A.M. and made a trip through the dormitories, where she said, "It needed no doctor to tell" her "that the children had been breathing poison." She interviewed doctors, matrons, and chaplains, listening to their side of every question, and watched the children while at work and at play. In order to compare them with other children of the same class differently reared, she went to see orphans boarded out in the country districts of Scotland and England, and the waifs and strays brought up in the Paris *Salles d'asiles*. To gain a knowledge of how the Metropolitan school children turned out in after life, she examined prison and reformatory statistics to see what proportion of the inmates came from pauper schools. In addition, as we have said, she traced by the aid of her friends the after careers of a large number of pauper girls who had gone into service. Everything she found out tended to strengthen her belief that children boarded out in families turned out far better than those massed together.

Briefly the results of her inquiries were these. The material with which the schools had to work was poor to begin with. This, however, could not altogether account for the prevailing inertia and apathy among the children, for their small size and their frequent ophthalmia and ringworm, since these diseases and characteristics were not to be found among the same class of children when boarded out in country homes under proper supervision, with good food, open air, family fostering, and normal conditions. When the girls left the pauper schools to go to service they showed no initiative. They had to be supervised and directed incessantly. They retained their school characteristics of weak health, stunted growth, and apathy, and frequently developed stubborn and violent tempers. They were apt to be irresponsible and untrustworthy, owing to having had no training in the duties of ordinary life. Though comparatively few drifted into prisons or reformatories, many ended on the streets.

To remedy these evils Mrs. Senior advised, first, that the casual children, who found long study hours irksome owing to their free, vagrant habits, be placed in a school by themselves where they could have much more out-door work, and where they would not contaminate the other children; second, that the orphans be boarded out in the country under proper supervision; and, third, that the deserted children be given a thorough training in housework and the care of babies. Such training might be facilitated, she thought, by combining the pauper infant establishments with the existing schools, and letting each nurse represent the mother of a family, having under her charge a certain number of girls whom she would instruct in nursing the younger children, and in cooking, sewing, sweeping, and even marketing and shopping.

Mrs. Senior was aware, however, that such changes could not soon be carried out. She therefore made many palliative suggestions as to ways in which the existing system might be improved. She recommended different school-room arrangements—desks of the right height, and so placed that the children would not face the light; in the dormitories, better ventilation, removal of clothing worn during the day, and less crowding; greater variety in the food, with less meat and more vegetables; many gentle gymnastics, and the looser clothing they would entail; more frequent changes of underclothing; and, above all, more breaks in the deadening monotony of the children's lives, such as rewards for good behaviour, slight changes in routine, and treats provided by outside benevolence. She speaks also of how the existing system might be rendered more efficient by the matrons having direct control over the servants, and by all the overworked officials having better pay and some enforced vacation.

Lastly Mrs. Senior considers what can be done to better the condition of the pauper girls when they leave school. Their supervision while under age and the choice of their positions should, she maintains, be confided to women and not to men. The matrons of the schools, however, are too busy to undertake such duties. She therefore recommends that the supervision of the girls from the various schools be given in charge of one central committee or board, which should officially employ competent women to visit the girls, and which should likewise oversee a registry office, and a temporary home for girls out of place.

All these carefully thought out plans will be found in the extracts from Mrs. Senior's report which we give in the appendix to this volume.

Mrs. Senior had put her whole soul into the work. The fresh air and happy home of her youth caused her to feel a burning pity for the little handicapped mites who had never had what had been bestowed so freely on herself. With failing health she had worked on to finish the report. It was the last thing she could do for these helpless little derelicts—her plea for them to the outside world.

The results of Mrs. Senior's work were far-reaching. The report was printed and copies found their way to the United States. Charity workers eagerly read it and adapted her sane views to their own problems. There was a tendency in America to supplant the boarding-out system already existing in many places, by big institutions. Mrs. Senior's report was of great value in combating the extension of that wholesale method of dealing with pauper children which had proved so unsatisfactory in England.

It is interesting to note that throughout the report Mrs. Senior constantly pleads for the family as the unit from which the child should start. How she would have battled against the ultra-modern theory that all children should be brought up by the state, may be easily imagined.

A strong supporter of all Mrs. Senior's views, was Miss Nightingale. She wrote the following letter immediately after she had read the manuscript of her report. At that time Mrs. Senior had just been appointed permanent inspector.

35 South Street,
Park Lane, W.,
January 5, 1874.

My dear Madam,—

I am so glad to hail you inspector; Officer of a Government Office—"Senior" Officer, as you strictly are (senior of one) *General of Infantry,* tho' they are only female infants, only poor-law female Infantry, that I hope you will allow me to address you as such.

My dear "Senior" General of Female Infantry,

I have read your papers once. You, or rather cruel fate, has given me such very short notice (and I am, at this time of year especially, so very busy with my infirmary Matron and other pearls) that I read your papers through in the cool of the morning, i.e. before it was light on Sunday and on this single perusal I must write in the cool of this Monday morning.

"Conclusion."

I agree with your "conclusion" so frantically that I agree with you more than you do with yourself. *That is, that Boarding out is the only way to save life and capacity in these poor children.* You have proved the case to demonstration nem. con. And then you are obliged to secede from your case: *Boards of Guardians* con., this is very hard.

N.B. Scrofula and its eldest child, ophthalmia, are greatly developed by merely bringing children—especially poor children—together. (You have no occasion to resort even to "clean" towels as a means of carrying "infection.") By subdividing (i.e. boarding out) you at once cut up this cause of ill-health and incapacity, root and branch, and clear the ground for training. You cannot do this in a large school, except at great cost.

This, I believe, stated roughly, is the conclusion of the whole matter—and in this I agree with you violently.

I incline to think that, if I were you, I would put the "Conclusion" at which you have arrived and which is quite beyond dispute, broadly: viz, that the shortest and best way is to set about at once the introduction of the *Boarding-out system in the country:* (Never in town unless under compulsion).

(A general must decide which point in the enemy's country she marches for: and then she must calculate *her* forces and *his* roads.)

Boarding-out solves all the difficulties.

You want only—houses to receive the children,
money to pay their board,
Inspector and Committee to see that everything is going on right.

The new School will supply education. Your poor little Infantry are poorly bred and poorly fed, and most, or all, more or less scrofulous. What they want of all things is: fresh air, good food, exercise, and personal kindness, and even with all this some will grow up to consumption: and many more to incapacity. To collect these children into large schools where they must be crowded and have impure air (the two conditions for the finest development of Scrofula and encouragement of incapacity) is simply dooming 8500 children of London to this prospect in different degrees. But with an inevitable inconsequence which is hard upon the General, she is compelled to fall back upon the *schools* and proposes to improve them. Much can be done, but it will be very costly. (Tho' not so costly as the having to maintain a large proportion of these 8500 and their offspring on the Rates.)

(1) *Superficial Area.*

You must have at least 50 square feet per child of Dormitory Area. (Superficial area is more important than cubic space or rather cubic space is more impor-

tant horizontally than vertically) besides suitable
means of warming, (not by gas) and ventilation, and
cleanliness including change of linen (*day* linen must
never be worn by *night*) and dirty clothes never to be
kept in Dormitory.

(2) There must be far more *sub-division*.
If this sub-division cannot be carried out by Board-
ing-out, it must be by "Home-schools or Cottage
Schools" of certainly not more than 30 children.
(Mixed ages.)
(You may say of *all* this poor little Infantry that
they are ill.
And certainly the danger and difficulty increases
as the square of the number.)

(3) The infant inmates of each "Home School"
should be certainly mixed with *older girls.*
Providence has arranged that each child of each
age should have a mother to itself, (for no woman
has 28 children between the ages say 5 and 6.) and
if unfortunately the mother is absent from death or
wickedness, the best thing we can do is to imitate
Providence's arrangement as nearly as we can.
(Experience e.g. teaches me every year, more and
more, that sick *children* are much better scattered
about in *adult* Sick Wards, than conglomerated in
Wards to themselves. *Every sick child* ought to have
a *nurse to itself;* this is impossible in the best *Children's*
Ward. But in *adult* Wards, the man or the woman
in the next bed, if well selected, will often take almost
entire charge of the adjacent child patient—even
most unlikely patients—young men of 20 or 25 will
do this, to the immeasurable benefit of both child and
adult.)
This is only an illustration from *Hospital* life but
the real way of benefiting *Pauper girls and infants* if

they cannot be boarded-out, would be to put them, *mixed up*, into a Cottage or *Home School* with a good nurse, matron and female servant; girls to learn housework and help mind infants: (as they would do in a good home.)

(Would it be quite impossible for them to have a cow, pig, and poultry?)

The three Rs do little to help poor law children. What is more wanted is: continued administration of the milk of human kindness, which is the appointed nutriment of Child-souls, and which no cow belonging to the *R* farm can yield.

(4) The General's proposed improvements most judicious, if you *must* have the present *Schools*. But all this will cost so much that Guardians will scarcely sanction it: *Boarding-out cheapest.*

(5) As regards *Casual* children, it is clear that there should be *some* power *somewhere* to keep the child in School, if the character and circumstances of the parents appear to render its going out unadvisable.

It is heart-rending to us sometimes in the Workhouse Infirmaries to have to give up a little child to a bad mother going out.

E.G.   We had a little girl 7 years old who used to go down on her little knees by herself, in the lavatory, praying that she might not forget the good words she had heard with us when she went out. (She knew already that her mother was a bad one.) . . .

God save the General.

Ever yours devotedly,

FLORENCE NIGHTINGALE.

The following letter from Miss Hill was written just after Mrs. Senior's report was printed:—

To Mrs. Nassau Senior.

September 20th, 1874.

. . . I was longing for news of you when the rumour reached me that your Report is really out. What that will really mean to you of suspense, anxiety, of doubt of what will be right under given circumstances to do or not to do, I can only imagine. But this I know, and should care for you to know,—that one, at least (one who is probably the sample of many), will be thinking of you with love and perfect trust. Whatever the newspaper critics, the interested officials, the angry partisans, may say, there are those who know that your work has been done with conscience, patience, singleness of eye and heart. There are those, too, who know that out of such work God will in His own good time bring results valuable to the world; that it is like good seed sown in good ground; and, though it may seem to die for a time, it will bear fruit. No momentary ebullition of feeling, no apparent failure, can ever confuse us as to this, we shall not be puzzled by having to wait for results;—nor will any minor points draw our attention from the fact that the work is thoroughly sound and good, governed by a right spirit; and it will vindicate itself as such, in the best of all possible ways, by achieving success, in the deepest sense of the much abused word "success."

You and I know that it matters little if we have to be the out-of-sight piers driven into the marsh, on which the visible ones are carried, that support the bridge. We do not mind if, hereafter, people forget that there *are* any low down at all; if some have to be used up in trying experiments, before the best way of building the bridge is discovered. We are quite willing to be among them. The bridge is what we care for, and not our place in it; and we believe that, to the end, it may be kept in remembrance that this is alone to be our object. But as we are human piers, conscious of our own flaws, we are apt to fear that, so far from forming strong supports, we may, through our own defects, be weak foundations for the bridge. We must remember always that God has been always pleased to build His best bridges with human piers, not angels, not working by miracles; but that He has always let us help Him, if we will, never letting our faults impede His purposes, when we struggled that they should not. . . .

Close on the publication of Mrs. Senior's report came her resignation. The following letter written at this time by Mr. Stansfeld explains itself:—

> STOKE LODGE,
> HYDE PARK GATE, W.,
> Wed. November 18, 1874.
>
> MY DEAR FRIEND,—
> I saw Mr. L. yesterday. . . .
> He does not think that any counter statements to yours are likely to be made, not because of your leaving, but because you have achieved so much in justification of your views, and of my choice of you, and because the press is with you; you will like to know this. . . .
> You leave therefore at least with flying colours, and with pleasant memories. You have been a success, I am justified, and the cause is helped, and a fruitful precedent admitted. . . .
> Affectionately,
> J. STANSFELD.

Mrs. Senior's resignation spread consternation among her friends. Miss Nightingale, who could never tolerate any one giving up work, wrote the following letter to her. She did not know that the woman to whom she sent it, was confined to her bed, and even there, working to the limit of her strength.

35 SOUTH STREET,
PARK LANE, W.
December 7, 1874.

MY DEAR MRS. SENIOR,—

I am so concerned at what I heard yesterday, that you had resigned Office, that I cannot help writing a word of sorrow. No personal grief has ever affected me more. . . . I look upon your resignation as a national misfortune. No one could have done what you have done: What you indeed have done during this brief space, against growing-up, grown-up female pauperism, a worse evil than a Cholera, or a War, or Popes, or Slavery, or Indian Zemindars, or any other evil we know. Consternation is my state. How many will remain paupers whom you would have saved. You were arrayed almost single-handed, a noble army of one, against this evil. And who will take your place? Who will redeem our generation? The outcry of the enemy shows what a club your gentle Hercules arm has wielded; and would you leave off till you had become Apollo Victor with his bow?

I only hope that ill-health is not the cause, or only a temporary cause, of this great disaster.

At all events, the great principle which you have initiated (without writing or platforming about it) namely, that woman must "inspect" woman, (and how will they do it?) cannot be again laid aside. Yet rather the resignation of the greatest Cabinet that ever was than yours.

I never thanked you for your Report, for it was un-

thank-able for.   I am so miserable that I can only
say further how much
> I am, dear Mrs. Senior,
> Your faithful and grateful servant,
> FLORENCE NIGHTINGALE.

I pray God that your successor may be one tenth of
you,

> F. N.

Mrs. Senior must have sent the above letter to Mr.
Stansfeld, as is evident from the following note:—

> ATHENÆUM CLUB,
> PALL MALL,
> 29 December, 1874.

MY DEAR FRIEND,—

C.* gives it against you about Florence Nightingale's letter: she likes it *from her* as she liked the
former ones, and she is a very acute and sharp critic
generally.

I instinctively feel rather with you; I think the form
is somewhat exaggerated and unsimple.   This is what
you felt, I think; but, on the other hand, on reflection,
though I had rather she wrote somewhat otherwise,
I think it easy to make too much of one's feelings in
the matter.

Remember she has lived so much a recluse, in bed;
communicating by pen, or often pencil, and paper,
and thus getting a mannerism quite unconsciously,
and that she does not see, or often write to you, and
that this is written in sudden hearing of the news.   It
is very natural that one so humble-minded as you
should be a little disturbed by such a letter, but "au
fond" she is right, and that say both of us. . . .
> Yours affectionately,
> J. STANSFELD.

* Mrs. Stansfeld.

The following letter from Florence Nightingale shows that she had forgiven Mrs. Senior her abdication. From the context, it seems that the " Report " had been reprinted in pamphlet form, and Miss Nightingale was most eager for its distribution.

35 SOUTH STREET
PARK LANE, W.
December 30, 1874.

MY DEAR MRS. SENIOR,—

... I will not prey upon you with any remarks, but will only say that from sixteen to eighteen is *the* dangerous age for girls, and therefore your Association-plan * at the end is peculiarly important.

If there is the least risk of "Copies enough" not "being bespoken" "to publish at all," pray let me "bespeak" twenty, or any larger number which may help to avért such a catastrophe.

I will not say either how deeply touched I was by your former letter, and indeed by your writing at all.

May God grant us that you have perfect rest now, and perfect recovery by and by. I prophesy that you will see of the "travail of your soul" and "be satisfied."　.

Yours ever overflowingly,
FLORENCE NIGHTINGALE.

After the Report was published, the lists in *The Times* were again opened to combatants, and many thronged to the tournament in haste to break a lance. Both Mrs. Senior's methods and conclusions were attacked, and we give portions of one editorial on the subject, and her rejoinder.

* Central Home for young servants.

EDITORIAL,—LONDON "TIMES," JANUARY 26, 1875.

Mr. T., as an old inspector, has done his duty to his office, and made a most important contribution to a serious question, in replying at great length to Mrs. Senior's Report against District Schools in favour of Boarding Out. We will frankly say that we wish we could think his observations less conclusive on the point than they appear to be. It is not merely that gallantry might prompt us to ask a little quarter for the lady belligerent, nor yet that there is a certain savour of old English life, cottage homes, and the like, in the Boarding-out alternative. The secret bias we are forced to confess for the lady is that she imports so much novelty, so much enterprise, and such originality of operation into her cause. In one matter she happens just to have done that which a thousand times over we have heard sensible people wish to see done, of course to no purpose. She has tried to follow out into their future careers many hundred girls from District Schools, to see how far that system is justified by its children. For this purpose she has employed a strong force of lady detectives, who follow up what scent they find, and, under the promise of secrecy and without giving any names, but only initials, contribute a mass of facts which Mrs. Senior appears to have thought decisive. . . . Her informants appear to have been too zealous in the discharge of their commission to observe those rules of accuracy and sound logic which even scandal should not wholly disregard. They, and for the matter of that, their employer, have not always taken the trouble to distinguish between *District* and *Workhouse* Schools when it is the former only that is in question, and when the worst that can be pressed against the latter is only a fresh argument for the former. They have not noticed at what age the child left school, how long she was there, or with what associates she had passed the interval, or, in a word, whether the result, if bad, could be tracked to the faults of the District School. But when all these ladies can say of a girl is that she was seen sitting on a step, or that she let her hair fall down her back, or did not stay long in a place, we must admit that the argument should not be left entirely in feminine hands. . . .

MRS. SENIOR
To THE EDITOR OF THE LONDON "TIMES."

. *Sir*,—While acknowledging the kindness of your intention, I cannot accept any plea of "gallantry" for being treated differently to any other of the Poor Law Inspectors. If either my methods of inquiry or my logic has led me to false conclusions, I am quite ready to acknowledge my error, but till error is proved much more conclusively than Mr. T. has proved it, I shall fight both for my methods and my conclusions.

I am officially and personally answerable for every one of them, with the same responsibility which Mr. T. feels for his statement. The women who worked for me were known and approved by the late President of the Local Government Board, but in every case I am responsible for their work. Mr. T. was invited to inspect the books in which their reports were entered, to meet them, and to examine the method on which they and I had worked. He declined. Another inspector and two chaplains of District Schools were similarly invited, with the same result. Another inspector, who accepted the invitation, satisfied himself that my conclusions had been arrived at neither hastily nor unfairly.

Before considering Mr. T.'s special views, it is neces-

sary to consider the position which he occupies.
When a man has introduced a great improvement in
administration and has for some thirty years superintended its working in detail, he must, necessarily,
be the last to admit the possibility of superseding his
work. Every consideration is due such a man personally, but that fact must be remembered when his
arguments are weighed.

He seems to suppose that I wish to do away with
the District and Separate schools and to substitute for
them the Boarding-out system. On both hands he is
mistaken. I suggested, not destruction, but change,
in the schools (Report, page 37), and I recommended
boarding-out for one only of the three classes into
which pauper children are divided—i.e. for the orphans,
not for the deserted nor for the casual class.

If I may judge of Mr. T.'s report by your article on
it, this ought to cut away the whole ground of his reply.
As for details, if you have accurately reproduced his
statements, they must be curiously wrong. For
instance, to say that I do not distinguish between
District and Workhouse Schools is an anachronism.
In the Metropolitan district, to which my inquiries
have been limited, workhouse schools have been
abolished for many years, and District and Separate
schools have taken their place.

The "scandal," as you are pleased to call it, concerning the girls designated "under initials" is divided
by me into two heads. The object of Appendix F
was "to ascertain how far the girls sent to service from
all the 16 metropolitan pauper schools in the years
1871 and 1872 were well conducted and efficiently
trained." The object of this inquiry was to ascertain
the value of the schools as training places for servants.

In Appendix G I sought to give an imperfect and
"approximate test" of the results of the education

upon a limited number of girls (51), all of whom had
left school in 1868, after not less than five years'
training therein.

In this Appendix (G) every particular of each
case is stated. Dates of admission and discharge,
age, cause of leaving, and every attainable particular
of her life since leaving. Yet you say we "have not
noticed at what age the child left school, how long
she was there, or with what associates she had passed
the interval."

Is this fair or true?

The details of "girls sitting on steps" and having
their "hair down their backs" are more or less trivial
items of a mass of circumstantial evidence which
completely proves its point. To isolate these details
from the rest, is the act of a singularly unjudicial mind.

Again, the girls might easily have good situations
if they were fit for them. In consequence of the low-
ness of their wages and their lack of friends, they are
much sought after, their outfit is good, and the general
demand for servants of their class is far ahead of the
supply. Yet you say "they cannot get good places."

. . . .

I hope you will forgive the length of this reply,
which is only a preliminary answer to Mr. T., whose
objections I trust in due time to be able to meet in
every particular with a satisfactory refutation.

I remain, Sir, your obedient servant,

JANE E. SENIOR.

LAVENDER-HILL S.W., January 26.

We conclude the chapter with a letter from "George
Eliot."

THE PRIORY,
21 NORTH BANK,
REGENTS PARK,
January 26, 1875.

MY DEAR FRIEND,—

I must indulge myself by telling you that we have been delighting today in your admirable letter to the *Times*, which is as strong and temperate as it could well be. After the vexation of seeing the *Times* article, which was of course written to order, your letter came as the most welcome news that the paper could bring us—much better than the choice of Liberal Leader. . . .

Believe me, dear friend,
Yours with deepest sympathy,
M. E. LEWES.

CHAPTER XIII.

LETTERS AND RECOLLECTIONS.

We begin this chapter with the last letter we have from Mr. Stansfeld. It is in marked contrast to the first. We can almost read the progress of his friendship in the signatures, so formal in the beginning, so cordial in the end. Following his letter, come two from another "soldier at the front," which show that Mrs. Senior, though "invalided home" in the Isle of Wight, still took a hand in the warfare, and was doing her best to help Miss Hill to get "open spaces" in London, and had evidently offered some piece of land of her own for the purpose.

MR. J. STANSFELD TO MRS. SENIOR.
STOKE LODGE,
HYDE PARK GATE, W.
July 28, 1875.

What a sweet letter you have sent me, and what a lovely sketch—really wonderful, I think. I feel quite sure that it is perfectly true, and the effect of distance beyond the water is quite charming.

I was indeed vexed to miss you and conscience stricken. I ought to have come before, but you don't chide (did you ever chide anybody?) but invent a pretty little excuse for me about "business first and pleasure afterwards." It is just like you, quite a temptation to behave ill. It is very good, and very sweet and unselfish of you, but I must not accept it; of course I could have found time. The real truth and reason is that I have been physically, and otherwise depressed too, and kept putting it off. I had rather confess it to you, and ask your forgiveness. How nicely W. planned the journey; I am so glad now to think of you being there at peace, it does indeed please me that you are so happy.

· · · · · · · · ·

Believe me, my very dear friend,
Yours affectionately,
J. STANSFELD.

MISS OCTAVIA HILL TO MRS. N. SENIOR.
AUGUST 19, 1875.

You will have heard from Charles of the sudden collapse of all our schemes for the purchase of the fields. The owners withdrew their offer after five days' notice. We were led to hope that this notice might be reconsidered, when the owner returned; but he confirms it, and tells us that we must consider the offer absolutely withdrawn, and refused even to receive a guarantee within a week for the full amount. I think the loss very great. The spirit of many of the people who helped us was so beautiful. I shall never forget *that*.

MISS OCTAVIA HILL TO MRS. N. SENIOR.
AUGUST 21, 1875.

We could almost have cried over your letter, dear, dear Janey; how delightful is your joy in doing what is blessed and helpful. I will think over the generous offer; but I believe now that we had better pause, for sufficient time to learn really which are now the best places available, and which those most needing space. . . . In short, Janey dearest, I will assuredly go and see your farm. But I must, I think, revise the whole area, and see where and how the space will tell most. And I ought now at once to go and finish my holiday in Ireland. I go with a ten-fold lighter heart for the love and generosity and sympathy of your letter and you need not fear that nothing will be done, because we don't act at once. . . .

We must now go back a few months to the early winter of 1874, when Mrs. Senior had resigned her post. It was at this time that Miss Sarah Forbes (in after years Mrs. Hastings Hughes) first came to Elm House, and we insert here her personal recollections of Mrs. Senior.

You ask me for the story of my acquaintance with Mrs. Senior. It is soon told.

My father had made a trip to England during the darkest days of the civil war between the North and South. He saw many influential men, and among others, the elder Mr. Senior, who invited him to spend one evening at his house. When the time came to go in to dinner, my father glanced about and, at once picking out the lady whom he wished to escort, stepped up to Mrs. Senior and offered her his arm. As they were going into the dining-room she said, without any preface, "I must tell you, Mr. Forbes, how heartily I sympathise with the North." He never forgot her words, coming as they did from a total stranger, yet with the ring of an old friend in them. His heart was won; and though their acquaintance was short, their friendship lasted for many years. Just before my father returned to America, he wrote to her.

"JUNE, 1863.

"Your warm sympathy touches a chord that seldom vibrates. I had thought myself proof against cold or heat and that I was entirely indifferent to English opinions and feelings, which I found so generally against us. Like the traveller in the fable, I can stand the pelting of the storm, but your sunshine draws off my cloak, and makes me aware that I am open to its cheering influence; and I tell it you, that you may know how much good you can do to others."

When I went to study water-colour painting in London, in 1874, my father gave me an introduction to Mrs. Senior. The first time I went to Elm House, she was too ill to see me; but the second time, I was shown upstairs to a small room, bare as a hospital ward, though with blazing fire and open window,— no carpet, no curtains, and a plain iron bedstead. Outlined against the pillows was the sweetest face I have ever seen. Masses of golden hair, bright as a young child's, shaded the delicate transparent features. The cheeks still had a tinge of clear colour. She wore a white lawn dressing sack and some sort of delicate lace on her head. She reminded me most of a Fra Angelico Angel, but her face was the face of one who had experienced suffering and overcome it. Weak tho' she was, there was not a trace of the sick-room atmosphere about her; and the glad smile, the eyes shining with welcome, the outstretched hands gave an instant sense of buoyant life.

She made me sit down beside her and tell all about the members of my family, young and old. She laughed heartily at my stories of nieces and nephews, and then matched them with tales about her own. I cannot describe the feeling of home it gave me. The hour of my visit flew as if by magic. When I was leaving, she called me to come and kiss her, and whispered, "God bless you, child."

After my first visit I went often, bringing her flowers and telling her tales of my London experiences. I had never been out of America before, and everything,

from old time Blue-coat boys to new time Pre-Raphael-
ites, struck me as interesting and intensely amusing.

Mrs. Senior used to laugh at the stories I told, until
the tears ran down her cheeks; then she would draw
a long breath, and say, "That did me more good than
pounds of medicine."

On Christmas day, 1874, I drove out to see her. It
was grey and rainy, and I was glad to get inside the
house, where her warm Christmas greeting made the
day bright. We fell to talking on the theatricals
with which my home people were celebrating the
holidays and of which they had written to me. She
said that before her illness her husband's little niece,
Amy Simpson and her brothers and sister, together
with the available Hughes nieces and nephews used to
gather at Elm House on Christmas. They had acted
charades and plays, and filled the place with frolic
and fun. Now that she was ill, however, she had
been forced to give it all up.

In the course of my visits I discovered that the best
rooms in the house were given over to the two grandmothers. Mr. Senior had a den in some secluded
spot, and her niece Emmy, her son, and the three boys
were scattered here and there. Beside these, Miss
Wilson, the daughter of an Indian officer, lived there
at this time, and her brother Hastings Hughes came
and went on his journeys to and from Spain. The
care of such a large household was, however, taken
off her shoulders by her son. I remember her once
saying of him, "He is both son and daughter to me."

Later in the winter of 1874–75, old Mrs. Hughes
went to live with Emily and Gerard in the Isle of Wight.
Their absence from Elm House occasioned Mrs.
Senior's move into a big, sunny room whence she
could see the garden. I always associate this room
with a talk we had there one day about George Eliot's

novels. In Mrs. Senior I had found to my joy an enthusiastic admirer of Scott and Emerson. But when we arrived at George Eliot there was a sharp division of opinion, for while I found "Adam Bede" and "Silas Marner" beyond praise, I could not stand "Middlemarch," and "Daniel Deronda." They seemed to me both heavy and dismal. When I openly expressed these views she smiled and said, "Ah, but they are so true to life, Sarah." I rebelled at such lives being considered typical, and plunged into stories of California travel, of the tall pines and great chasms and water-falls of the Yosemite, and the miles and miles of wild, uncultivated land.

"There is no end to the land in your wonderful country," she said and then added, "it is so open; you seem to have no skeletons in your closets in America."

I answered that there might be some, but that such unpleasant house-mates had never come into my experience.

"I believe you," she said. "Life is simpler there."

Although Mrs. Senior did none of the actual house-keeping, her room was the centre of family activities. One day her little niece would come in clad in her red cape, on her return from school. Another day I would find Harry housed with a cold by his aunt's bedside. Again, old Madame Senior would wander in, wanting a bit of change and amusement after the tedium of her own room. She was nearly ninety and very deaf. She would ask endless questions about the contents of her daughter-in-law's work basket. Mrs. Senior's voice was weak, and she must have found answering hard; yet I never heard a trace of impatience in the sweet tones, and a tender, amused smile played about her mouth as she replied to each query in turn.

One day an inspiration seized the old lady, and she came hurrying in. "Jeanie! Jeanie! There is a

picture of a naked woman in my room. It is either
Eve or Venus, I don't know which. Would you like
it in here?"

A flash of fun danced in the eyes of the younger
woman. Her gentle negative, however, was free from
the least hint which could have wounded the elder
lady.

I saw more or less also of Mrs. Hughes before she
moved to the Isle of Wight. She had retained her
love of country work even in a suburb of London. She
managed to keep a cow, and oversaw the vegetable
garden, which she showed the stranger with pardon-
able pride. She kept her little grand-daughter much
with her, and taught her needle-work and common
sense, just as she had taught her own daughter nearly
forty years before.

How this complicated household was harmonised was
plain enough to those who watched the family under
Mrs. Senior's leadership. She herself, however, never
regarded the task as a hard one and did it as simply
and serenely as she did everything else in life. A
bright west wind, so tempered as to ruffle no one,
seemed always blowing through the house.

After a talk with Mrs. Senior, I came away with the
feeling that I had never met any one who took life
with such happy courage. Her creed seemed to be a
gallant acceptance of whatever came, mingled with
a determination never to burden any one else with
such sorrows as crossed her path. She did not speak
of her pauper work to me, preferring to hear of happy
homes and people able to enjoy life. I never heard
from her of the loss of her four brothers, three of whom
died in early youth and one in the prime of life, nor did
she speak of the likelihood of her own death. Once
she said that she was not afraid to die—it would only
be like passing from one room to another.

She abhorred the "pitiers of themselves," and had no patience with those who preferred misery to brave and decisive action. She once wrote, "It is contemptible to sit down to be a martyr, when by a little courage you can be a saint triumphant, and help others to higher ground, rather than let them light the faggots to burn you!"

In June I went to see Mrs. Senior for the last time before returning to America. After a short talk, it was time to go. A look at the lovely face, a kiss and a low spoken blessing from her, and I left the room, never to see her again.

After Miss Forbes' departure Mrs. Senior wrote often to her, telling her the latest pieces of family news. From these letters we can gather the history of the months between July, 1875, and January, 1877.

The first of Mrs. Senior's letters from which we quote is dated November, 1875. She had spent the preceding summer at Colwell Bay with her mother, having found the noise of the trains which ran past Elm House terribly annoying. Her son had planned the move, as has been seen from Mr. Stansfeld's letter. In the autumn she returned to London somewhat improved in health.

FROM MRS. SENIOR TO MISS FORBES.

ELM HOUSE,
November 8, 1875.

DEAR SARA,—

... I have been badly the last ten days with bad fits of pain. I am told that these attacks do not lessen my chances of recovery, but they are wearying and leave me feeling shattered. Still, on the whole, I get on, and I know that Patience is the best cure. . . .

In answer to a letter from Miss Forbes commenting on the desire of young Englishmen to go to the far West and start life on a sheep or cattle ranch, Mrs. Senior writes:—

ELM HOUSE,
24 December, 1875.

... It so happens that to a great many of us has come the greatest desire to return to a simple, primitive *out-door* life and to live by hand labour rather than by head labour, and I welcome this impulse because I am certain that for many generations the brains of men have been at full stretch in the terrible competition of this over-crowded country, and that health is deteriorating in consequence. The children are not clever and the physical type degenerates. A return to mother earth and out door pursuits seems to me to be clearly indicated as the cure. . . .

In a letter written in the January of the following year to Mr. Forbes thanking him for a barrel of apples and "Parnassus," a collection of Emerson's favourite poems, Mrs. Senior says:—

Mr. Emerson's book will be a great delight to me. There is no one living whom I would like to know so much as Mr. Emerson. I have the greatest reverence and sympathy for him, and you could not send me any book that I should value so highly.

. . . .

I often amuse myself by thinking of all the great and good people with whom I hope to make friendship in the next world. I can hardly hope to know Emerson in this life, for I see less and less hope of going to your country as I had so wished, and I fear that Emerson will not come here again. . . .

In February she wrote to Miss Forbes:—

ELM HOUSE, 1876.

DEAR SARA:

. . . We've all lost money lately and are drawing in as much as possible until our estate at Willesden begins to sell for building land. . . .

We may, perhaps, have to leave this house and go to a smaller one, which would not "scare" me in the least. But I don't know yet. We have let the garden to a nurseryman which saves us a good deal.

On this subject she wrote again in March, 1876:—

. . . We are trying to let this house. I have had a loss of income, and this place is now too expensive for us, and we must get a house well within our means. It is a bother always, to uproot and have the worry of a move, but anything is better than the risk of spending more than one's income. On this point I am entirely of Mr. Micawber's opinion. In "David Copperfield," do you remember? It is something to this effect: "annual income, 30£ 0s. 0d.; expenditure, 30£ 0s. 6d.—result, *Misery*. Expenditure per annum, 29£, 19s. 6d. result *Happiness*, so we are going to move into a much cheaper house. We have heard of one to suit us perfectly at Chelsea by the river, if we can get rid of this house before the other is let over our heads.

Old Mrs. Senior will live with us still, for we have promised her a home with us as long as she lives. . . .

Little Harry (Hastings' youngest boy) will remain with us and continue to attend Westminster School. . . . Emmy and Gerard already live with mother (in the Isle of Wight), as Gerard is to be an artist and Mr. Watts is undertaking his education, and Watts is more at Freshwater than in London.

From the following letter from Mrs. Hughes to Miss Forbes, we see that Mrs. Senior's improvement in health began in the spring of 1876:—

MY DEAR SARA,—

. . . I know how glad you will be to hear that I think my dear child is gaining ground. I spent six happy weeks with her at Xmas, and was delighted to observe how much her nervous system is strengthened, and improved since you saw her. Noises that used to overcome and distress her beyond endurance, now pass unheeded, or rather enjoyed, for she rather likes to listen to my little grandchild's practice in her room! This I think a sure sign that her strength is greatly improved. Since I returned home, six weeks ago, I have been living quite alone, for I left little Emmy with her aunt, that she might be under the eye of the dentist. . . . Hastings and his three boys are quite well, the eldest, Willie, going every morning into the city and working with his father till six o'clock in the evening. It is not a very enjoyable employment for a young boy, but Willie makes no complaint and works away diligently. . . .

Believe me dear, affectionately yours,

MARGARET E. HUGHES.

In the following letter we have the last reference to the "Uncle Tom" who had taken such tender care of his niece on the Italian journey nearly thirty years before.

MRS. SENIOR TO MISS FORBES.

APRIL 15, 1876.

DEAR SARA,—

. . . Mother is not at her home now. . . . She is nursing her old brother of 88, who has been very ill at Bournemouth. · A violent illness at that age usually kills, but this wonderful old uncle has recovered, except that he is weakish and does not like to have mother leave him.

On account of the loss of property, spoken of in the foregoing letters, the Seniors took the house at Chelsea. While the move was being accomplished, Mrs. Senior went to her mother's home in the Isle of Wight, from whence she wrote to Miss Forbes:—

COLWELL, YARMOUTH, ISLE OF WIGHT.
July 1, 1876.

DEAR SARA,—

. . . We have got a much smaller and cheaper house, which I like better than the large one. It is less anxiety and trouble now I am ill, and by living quietly we shall get on. . . .

Hastings has gone into a little lodging with his boys, we had furniture to spare and made it "comfy" for him. He and his lads do all the chores and cooking and are as contented and happy as larks. . . .

I delight myself by poring over Lowell. Walter and I agree there is no living poet like him.

From another letter we quote the following encouraging news:—

COLWELL, ISLE OF WIGHT,
18 August, 1876.

I am wonderfully better for this glorious sunshine and heat. I can't tell you how different I feel. I really think now, of some day being better again and perhaps well enough to visit my kind friends in the wonderful country. . . .

On her return to Chelsea Mrs. Senior wrote to Miss Forbes:—

2 NOVEMBER, 1876.

MY DEAR SARA,—

I have been a sad long time answering your letter, but I have had my dear old mother most seriously ill for more than a month. So I neglected everything and every one but her. She came to pay me a little visit and fell ill almost immediately. I was so thankful that she was ill here rather than at Colwell, for she had the Doctor she is accustomed to and a professional nurse.

She has recovered in a most wonderful way, and as soon as she was well enough to travel, Hastings took her to Colwell, that is three days ago, and I have excellent accounts of her, thank God. If she will but believe that she is old and must be careful of herself, I believe she will do very well, but altho' in her 80th year she thinks she may live like a young woman. . . . I am wonderfully better than I was six months ago. I really believe that I shall get strong again in a year or so. If so, I shall try to get back to my old work, if the liberals are in then, not only for the love of it but also for the pay. But I fear that the liberals have little chance of being in for years to come, for the conservatives have so disgraced us in this Turkish business, and the country is so sleepy that it is unequal to rousing itself to turn them out.

I am quite disgusted with my country, thoroughly ashamed that we should support those unimprovable tyrants and bigots, the Turks, against people who only want a little freedom and security to become a fine people. I should like to see the Turks driven out of Europe, and Constantinople held by the Jews (or any neutral people). Anything to get rid of the Turk. . . .

In the same month, Mrs. Senior wrote to Mr. John M. Forbes as follows:—

98 CHEYNE WALK, CHELSEA, LONDON,
Nov. 28, 1876.

MY DEAR MR. FORBES,—

Even before I got your letter, I had been full of sympathy & interest in your Presidential Election. . . . I sympathise with you most deeply now, as you know I did in the terrible time when I had the pleasure of making your acquaintance. The march of the world is, daily, a greater and greater mystery to me. The wrong seems so often triumphant. But I keep my faith in the ultimate triumph of good over evil, by remembering that what we see is only such a tiny segment of an inconceivably large circle, that we must not lose heart, but wait & trust and work on, without discouragement; as you do.

. . . .

Give my kind love to all who remember me, & believe me, etc.

JEANIE E. SENIOR.

Here follows the last letter Mrs. Senior wrote to Miss Forbes:—

COLWELL, YARMOUTH, ISLE OF WIGHT,
January 4, 1877.

MY DEAREST SARAH,—

. . . I am here by the doctor's orders, not that I am ill, on the whole I am wonderfully better and the doctor seems sure of my recovery, but in London there are so many friends who call to see me and whom I don't like to refuse that I get overdone almost without knowing it, until the pressure is taken off. The first week I was here I felt quite collapsed. But what

can one do? One can't send away a friend one *wants*
to see, just because one has seen others. The doctor
was clever enough to see what, at the time, I did not
feel; and so I came here for Xmas with Hastings, his
four children and Walter, much to the joy of my dear
old mother. Mrs. Senior went to her daughter and
Nassau remained at home alone which is his idea of
perfect happiness. If he had his wish, he says he
should never again sleep a night out of his own house.

Walter has gone back to his law, of course, and
Hastings and his eldest lad have gone to their business,
but the three children still are left here to rejoice my
soul. . . .

God bless you, my dear child, and give you and all
of your dear ones every blessing in the coming year.

Ever yours affectionately

J. E. S.

CHAPTER XIV.

LETTERS TO EMILY HUGHES—MRS. SENIOR'S
DEATH.

We now turn back from the early winter of 1877,
when Mrs. Senior's health appeared to be improving
so hopefully, to the autumn of 1875. She had returned
from Colwell Bay to Elm House, but her illness was
then no better, and she was still confined to her bed
with the bad attacks of pain mentioned in her letter
to Miss Forbes. On November 8 she wrote the
following letter to her niece Emily:—

DARLING,—

Thank you for the receipt and the letter. . . . You
must not forget every Saturday to look through
Gerard's clothes as well as your own, and to take all
that need mending and put them into your mending
basket to be done in the week. His socks you must
carefully mend, and see that his buttons are right.

I am glad that you and Gerard like "Old Mortality."
I hope that you and Gerard read it aloud to Granny,
instead of letting her read it aloud to you, as she is
sure to do because she is so good and unselfish unless
you and Gerard insist on taking your share of reading
aloud.

I hope you both work hard with "Jeanne," * and
that you and Gerard practice violoncello and piano
pieces.

I hope your red cloak will fit you, dear child. I had

* The German governess.

MARGARET ELIZABETH HUGHES AND HER GRANDDAUGHTER,
EMILY.
(*From a photograph, taken 1880.*)

to unpick all that Mrs. Palmer had done and as I had
not you to measure by had to go by guesswork. . . .

Love to Gerardy and Jeanne, and much to yourself
darling.

EVER YOUR OWN OLD AUNTIE.

The next letter was written some months later.
Her brother Hastings Hughes and his boys were taking
advantage of their family misfortunes and, instead of
being fittingly woebegone, were heartily enjoying
themselves "camping out" in lodgings at Bark Place
and doing all their own work. Emmy went to visit
this festive company to her great satisfaction. Need-
less to remark she was instantly privileged to become
"head cook and bottle washer." While playing this
rôle the small girl received the following letter from
her aunt:—

COLWELL BAY, ISLE OF WIGHT,
July 13, 1876.

MY DARLING MAID OF ALL WORK,—

What a delightful letter you have sent your two
old women.

It has been such a pleasure to us. I think I must
send you your other cool pinafore and your cooking
apron. You will need cool things to do your work
in. . . . Walter says you are to stay ten days. What
a happy girl you will be.

Now about your beefsteak. No wonder they were
dry if you put them in the oven! If you have to do
this again, you must put the steaks in a breakfast-cup,
or tiny basin. Then you must fill a saucepan about
a third full of warm water (the saucepan must be big
enough for the cup which holds the meat to stand in

when the lid of the saucepan is on). You must into this saucepan of warm water stand the cup with the meat in it and put a tablespoonful of water and a small pinch of salt in with the meat in the cup. Then put on the saucepan lid tight and stand it in the oven till it is needed for dinner. It will not be dried up.

To make your steaks or chops tender, you must lay them on a clean bit of wood and beat them hard about eight times on each of their sides with a meat chopper or any clean, heavy bit of iron that you have (clean the iron well both before and after), then lay the meat in a clean dish and put six or eight drops of salad oil on each bit of meat, then turn each bit over and put four or five drops on the other side of each bit of meat and let the meat lie in the oil a few hours, if possible. When you put the meat to the fire, keep it close to the fire (the fire must be bright) for three or four minutes, then turn the other side of meat to the bright fire for three or four minutes. The heat being very fierce seals up the gravy. Then draw back the gridiron until it is three or four inches from the bars, and let the steak finish cooking.

The day you went away Dyer, Maggie and Arthur and Jeanne drew me over to see Mr. Prinsep. I enjoyed the outing much and was greatly amused to see all the chickens. The carriage was drawn up under the verandah by Mr. Prinsep's sitting room and I went in and paid him a half hour's visit. He has a cough, dear old man, but I hope it is not very bad. He will be 85 on Saturday. . . .

Yesterday I went up to the corner of the fort towards Totlands. It was the most heavenly day. I stopped there for an hour looking at the lovely view. It is too far for dearest Gran to walk. I wish we had a bath chair for her like Mr. Prinsep's.

I am longing for the donkey. Dyer has got the

harness arranged. If you had come back we had arranged to go to tea on the Downs on Saturday. But I shall wait for your return for that. Gran and the tea will go up in the pony chaise.

It is such heavenly weather! So hot, the sea like glass! I long for all my dear Bark Placers to be here.

The house is very dull without our little sunshine and I miss you terribly before breakfast, when I read my Bible all alone. God bless you my darling. I love to think how happy you all are at Bark Place. Our love to all.

EVER YOUR LOVING OLD AUNT J.

By September, Emmy was back in the Isle of Wight, and Mrs. Senior in Chelsea, from whence she wrote the two letters which follow. From the first we see how much her health had improved since the year before.

4 LINDSAY HOUSES,
CHELSEA,
1 September, 1876.

DARLING CHILD,—

Thank you for your nice letter. I think that bathing in such a rough sea (not ruff, remember a ruff is a frill round the neck) must be very disagreeable. . . .

It will be a great treat to me to have you here, darling. It would be well to bring up the book of Tunes which you play with Gerard that I may hear if you play them right. Also your two Mozart duets to play with me, for the doctor allows me to sit up to the piano an hour a day, and I shall love to play with you. If it is fine on Sunday, I am going to the river with your father and Willie. The doctor thinks it will be very nice for me to get a day out of doors. I was very much amused as I drove to Mr. Muridges',

with looking at the shops. I have not seen anything
like big shops for two years.

I wish you'd bring me up any drawings that you've
done since Gerard and you have worked together.

God bless you, my sweet.

EVER YOUR OWN AUNT J.

Love to the dear boys.

MRS. SENIOR TO HER NIECE EMILY.

98 CHEYNE WALK, CHELSEA,
November 11, 1876.

DARLING CHILD,—

Mr. Taylor (the doctor) says that alcohol is only to
be used as medicine for very old people or when people
have some sort of illness, so do not drink beer. If
Granny wishes you to have anything but water, have
a little milk. But the best thing you could drink
would be water from the spring by the shore. I wish
you would every day fetch up a jug, and then Granny
could have some too. . . . I like to hear about your
sums and lessons, darling, but what expensive cheese!
3 lbs. ⅛ to cost 6£ 8s. 6d. I am glad I can get it
cheaper at the Aylesbury dairy. I shan't go to Colwell and buy cheese of you, Miss! . . .

How is Puff? or have you changed his name? I
hope you are very careful about cleaning and feeding
and watering him.

Gran says you wait on her nicely. That is right,
darling, you cannot do too much for the dearest Gran
who has been mother and Gran also to you since you
were born.

Remember, by the by, that the best foot warmer
for you, young creature, is not extra socks but extra
skipping and running and plenty of *oily food* and
some sugar. Ask Louey to fry your potatoes in
plenty of dripping and ask Gran to give you jam and

a bit of chocolate to eat with dry bread when you go out at twelve, not enough to spoil your dinner of course. You'd better, on Sunday, write a nice long letter to Bark Place. God bless you, darling.

EVER YOUR OLD LOVING AUNTIE.

These letters would seem to show a real advance towards recovery, and her friends began to feel relieved. She was taken out in a rowboat on the Thames several times, and enjoyed every moment of her little excursions. She had even resumed her music and though her voice was weak it was still exquisitely sweet and clear. One Sunday evening she sang the "Angels' Serenade" by Braga, her nephew Willie taking the violin part, and those who heard her sing said it was so tender and lovely that the tones were never forgotten.

Then, with no warning, she suddenly became worse, and in a few days "passed from one room to another," all those she most loved being near her when the door was opened.

We conclude this chapter with a letter which Miss Octavia Hill wrote to one of her friends.

MARCH 21, 1877.

Did you know Mrs. Nassau Senior? . . . I sit waiting for the telegram that shall tell me that she is gone from among us. I feel stunned; for I had a large hope from her vigorous constitution; and now this relapse is strange. She was, among my many friends, one of the noblest, purest-hearted, bravest to accept, for herself and all she loved, pain, if pain meant choice of highest good; with an ardent longing to serve, a burning generosity, which puts us all to shame. More-

over she loved me as few do; and I her; and, when
I think that I can go to her no more, I dare not think
of what the loss will be.   But neither dare I grieve;
she seems too high, too near, too great, to grieve for
or about; . . . if one keeps one's spirit true and quiet,
and in tune with the noblest part of the absent loved
ones, strange voices come across the silence, convic-
tions of how they feel, and what they would say, if
they could, to our listening hearts. . . .

CHAPTER XV.

WORK CARRIED ON.

"Built of tears and sacred flames,
And virtue reaching to its aims;
Built of furtherance and pursuing,
Not of spent deeds, but of doing."
Emerson.

After Mrs. Senior died Lady Ritchie wrote to her mother:—

How she has blessed us all, helped us, comforted us. Some people seem to me like messengers from God, already come, and she is one of these. . . . Dearest Mrs. Hughes, I can only tell you I love Jeanie and ask you to let me be something to you for her beloved and noble sake.

This letter gives the spirit that animated all Mrs. Senior's friends. Every one of them wished to honour her memory with living deeds. Those who most intimately knew her plans and wishes, set themselves at once to further them in every possible way.

Miss Octavia Hill took upon herself the support of an orphan child whom she boarded out in memory of Mrs. Senior. Walter Senior, together with other friends, formed the "Association for Placing Orphans in Private Families," which still boards out five or six children every year in carefully selected homes.

Another, and far more important association, to

which Mrs. Senior had given impulse and life was the "Metropolitan Association for the Befriending of Young Servants." This had been started shortly after the publication of the Report, and laid out along the lines suggested in it. The Association grew with startling rapidity, owing to the devotion of Mrs. Senior's friends. In 1897 it took charge of nearly eight thousand young servants, and had close upon one thousand ladies "engaged in befriending them." The Lord Mayor of London now attends the meetings, and assists in the distribution of prizes to those girls who have been most faithful in their work. We cannot do better than close this memoir with Lady Ritchie's account of the Association, quoted from "Upstairs and Downstairs."

Lady Ritchie gives a longer story of the address of an ex-speaker of the House of Commons to the Lord Mayor of London than we have space for here. Briefly, this gentleman said that not only was the Association in charge of eight thousand girls from the pauper schools, but that sixteen hundred other friendless girls were in its care. The girls were looked after when in place by the ladies, and when out of place came to the central house of the Association until suitable homes could be found. All were registered and their careers carefully noted. The guardians of the pauper schools were, for the most part, working with the Association. The cost of all this care amounted to fifteen shillings for each girl.

Lady Ritchie goes on:—

.   .   .   .

15*s.* each does not seem a very exorbitant subscription for the results achieved—8000 little charmaids helped and comforted, and scolded and advised, and kept from incalculable temptation and wretchedness; sheltered when homeless, nursed in sickness, encouraged and comforted in every way.

The first office the Association ever opened was at Chelsea. It is a friendly little place, which takes a benevolent interest in the various domestic fortunes and misfortunes of the neighbourhood. If you go there of a Monday morning you may find a room full of customers of various sizes, and an almost providential adjustment of different requirements. But indeed most of these offices are alike. There was one at B. where I spent an hour the other morning admiring the cheerful presence of mind of the manager, who seemed able to combine all sorts of difficult requirements.

"Well, you see," a stout lady was saying confidentially, "I'm so much alone evenings, my husband being out with the carriage, I want a girl for comp'ny as much as anything else. I don't want no housework from her. I want her to do any little odd jobs I can't attend to myself, and to mind the children. That was a good little girl enough you sent me, Miss Y.; but dear me, she was always crying for her mother. I let her out on Mondays, and Wednesdays, and Fridays; but she wanted to go home at night as well, and now she says she won't stay."

"It's her first place, m'am," says Miss Y. "They are apt to be homesick at first, but here is a very good little girl who has no home, poor child, she is quite alone. Fanny, my dear, should you like to live with Mrs. —— and take care of her nice little children?"

Smiling Fanny steps forward briskly, and off they

go together. Then a pretty young lady, fashionably
dressed in fur tippet, begins—

"That girl was no good at all, Miss Y. Such a
dance as she led me! She came and gave me a reference miles away, and ill as I was I dragged myself
there; and when I got to the house she herself opened
the door, and said her mistress was out and was never
at home at all. I said at once, 'You don't want to
come to us, and you haven't the courage to say so,'
and then she shut the door in my face and ran away!
The fact is, many don't like houses with apartments.
Our first floor is vacant at present, but I hope it will
soon be let; and I should be so glad to find a girl who
would come at once, and who knows something of
cookery, though my mother always likes to superin-
tend in the kitchen."

"There is a young woman who says she can cook,"
says the superintendent doubtfully, "but there seems
to be some difficulty about getting her character. Do
you think we had better write to your mistress for it,
my dear?"

A poor, fierce, wildbeast-looking creature, who had
been glaring in a corner, here in answer growls, "I
don't know, I'm sure."

"Why did you leave?" says the young lady.

"Cos she had such a wiolent temper," says the girl,
looking more and more ferocious.

"That is a sad thing for anybody to have," said
the young lady gravely.

At this moment a boy puts his head in at the door.
"Got any work for me?" says he.

"No, no," cry all the girls together. "This isn't
for boys; this is for females," and the head disappears.

"Well and what do *you* want?" says the superintendent, quite bright and interested with each case
as it turns up, and a spruce young person, who had

been listening attentively, steps forward and says, looking hard at the young lady in the tippet,

"I wish for a place, if you please, m'am, with a little cooking in it, where the lady herself superintends in the kitchen—a ladies' house that lets apartments, if you please; and I shouldn't wish for a private house, only an apartment house." At which the young mistress, much pleased, steps forward, and a private confabulation immediately begins.

While these two young people are settling their affairs a mysterious person in a veil enters and asks anxiously in a sort of a whisper, "Have you heard of anything for me, Miss? You see (emphatically) it is something so *very* particular that I require, quite out of the common."

"Just so," says Miss Y., "I won't forget."

"Don't forget, and you won't mention the circumstances to anyone," says the other, and exits mysteriously with a confidential sign.

Follows a smiling little creature, with large round eyes.

"Well," said Miss Y., who is certainly untiring in sympathy and kindness, "is it all right? are you engaged, Polly?"

"Please, Miss, I'm *much* too short," says the little maiden.

As we have said, it is not only the district girls who apply at these offices; all the young persons of the neighbourhood are made welcome by the recording angels (so they seem to me), who remember their names, invite them to take a seat on the bench, produce big books where their histories, necessities, and qualifications are all written down, and by the help of which they are all more or less "suited." Besides a home, a mistress, a kitchen to scrub, if they behave themselves they are also presented with a badge and

honourable decoration, fastened by a blue ribbon, and
eventually they are promoted to a red ribbon, the
high badge of honour for these young warriors. And
though some people may smile, it is, when we come
to think of it, a hardly-earned distinction, well de-
served as any soldier's cross. What a campaign it
is for them—a daily fight with the powers of darkness
and ignorance, with dust, with dirt, with disorder.
Where should we be without our little serving girls?
At this moment, as I write by a comfortable fire, I
hear the sound of a virtuous and matutinal broom in
the cold passages below, and I reflect that these 8000
little beings on our books are hard at work all over
London and fighting chaos in the foggy twilight of a
winter's morning.

[From *Punch*, April 7, 1877, by Tom Taylor.]

IN MEMORIAM

Jane Elizabeth Senior.

Not for the bright face we shall see no more,
    Not for the sweet voice we no more shall hear;
Not for the heart with kindness brimming o'er,
    Large charity, and sympathy sincere.

These are not things that ask a public pen
    To blazen its memorial o'er her name;
But, that in public she wrought with men,
    And faced their frowns, and over-lived their blame.

Yet never swerved a hair's breadth from the line
    Of woman's softness, gentleness, and grace;
But brought from these an influence to refine
    Rough tasks and squalid, and there leave its trace.

Honour to him who in a sneering age,
   Braved quip and carp and cavil, and proclaimed
A woman's fitness pauper needs to gauge,—
   In purpose strong, in purity unshamed.

For paupers too have sex: the workhouse walls
   Hold mothers, maidens, and girl babes, on whom
A woman's eye with woman's insight falls,
   Sees its own ways for sunlight to their gloom.

And so this noble and brave lady turned
   From glad life, luxury, and thronging friends
That hung on her sweet voice, and only yearned
   To guide her holy work to useful ends.

But Death to Life begrudged her, striking down
   The task unfinished from her willing hands,
Leaving to women yet to come the crown
   Of her left life's-work, that for others stands.

Then lay and leave her in her quiet grave,
   Where the sun shines undimmed, the rain falls clear,
And birches bend, and deodaras wave
   Evergreen arms of welcome o'er her bier.

APPENDIX

EDUCATION OF GIRLS IN PAUPER SCHOOLS—

REPORT ON, BY MRS. NASSAU SENIOR.

INTRODUCTORY.

January 1st, 1874.

Sir,

In January 1873 you told me that you wished to have the *woman's view* as to the effect on girls of the system of education at pauper schools. You asked me if I would undertake to visit the workhouse schools, and report to you the conclusions at which I arrived. . . .

I have given my attention almost exclusively to questions affecting the physical, moral and domestic training at the schools. I have not attempted to judge of the scholastic work, as I required all the time allowed me, for looking into the matters on which I knew that you more especially desired the judgment of a woman.

I divided the inquiry into two parts,—

1st. As to the present working of the system in the schools.

2d. As to the after career of the girls who had been placed out in the world.

1st, of my inquiries as to the working of the system in the different schools. The plan on which I pro-

ceeded was this:—I visited the 17 metropolitan schools
once, postponing the more particular investigation of
each school to a later period. When this round of
visits was completed I went to see some country
districts in England and Scotland, in order that I
might compare the physical condition of the children in
our metropolitan schools with that of children placed
in private families. (See Appendix A.)

I also visited orphanages, industrial schools, kindergartens, reformatories, &c. in England, and Scotland,
and in Paris I went over some of the most important
salles d'asile and orphanages, and saw some children
boarded out in families.

2. The second part of my inquiry set me upon
looking for such traces of the girls who had been
educated in the schools as might be found in the
records of various institutions into which, in case of
failure, they might have drifted.

My next endeavour was to ascertain the history of
the girls who had been placed in service from the
schools in the last two years.

I obtained at the schools the names and addresses
(more or less exact) of about 650 girls, those, namely,
who had been placed out in service during the years
1871 and 1872 in all parts of London and its suburbs,
and the history of each girl, as derived from the books
or otherwise, was sought to be verified by personal
investigation. The very great number of visits to be
made and inquiries to be set on foot involved in this
investigation, could not within the time allowed, be

undertaken by myself personally, but the work was effectually carried out by several indefatigable friends. The results of the whole inquiry into the history of these 650 girls will be found in Appendix F.

But, after all, I was not satisfied that I had yet arrived at the truest test of the merits of the system. The different effect of good and bad training could, I thought, completely prove itself only in the long run. A nearer approximation to a perfect test would be afforded by tracing the career of a number of girls who had left school five years before (in 1868), after having been not less than five years at school.

I inquired personally into the history of 51 of these girls. The time at my disposal obliged me to confine myself to girls from three of the metropolitan schools. The result of this inquiry will be found in the Appendix G.

The girls are designated by initials instead of by their names; first, because it seems clearly unadvisable that individual girls should be identified by particulars recorded of them; and, secondly, because a good deal of the information was obtained from mistresses with the expectation on their part that though their statements of facts would be recorded and considered in arriving at my conclusions, still they would not be personally referred to, or in any way compromised by the information they had afforded.

The information, therefore, which is classified and tabulated in Appendices F. and G., must be taken

for what, under these conditions and circumstances,
it may be held to be worth. . . .

The observations and suggestions resulting from
the whole inquiry will fall under two principal heads,
according as they refer to the life of the children—

(*A.*) in School, or (*B.*) in the world.

A. in School.   I.   Classification of children.
                   II. Sanitary conditions.
                   III. Moral and industrial training.
B. in the world.   I.   Choice of situations.
                   II. Supervision.
                   III. Guardianship.
                   IV. Protection when out of place.
                        Conclusion.

A. I. CLASSIFICATION.

.   .   .   .

The reasons given for continuing the present system,
rather than attempting any new classification with
a view to separating the permanent from the vagrant
children are, that the permanents bring the casuals
rapidly into order without suffering any deterioration
themselves from the contact, and that if the permanent
element were removed and trained separately, the
schools devoted to casuals only, would become so
demoralised that the children in them would not
have a chance of turning out well, and also that good
masters and matrons would not easily be found to
undertake the management of a school in which there

was no permanent element. I have heard it said that such a school would be a Hell on earth.

The difficulties of managing the pauper schools, even under the present system, are so great that one can heartily sympathise with the dread expressed by some of the officers of a change which, it appears to them, would add to their difficulties. We are none the less bound, however, to look simply at the question whether the presence of the casual children does or does not cause any moral deterioration to the permanent children, as being those whose interests are chiefly at stake in the matter.

To the eye of a visitor the outward order of the schools is in most respects perfect, and it seems generally agreed that the presence of a mass of children already drilled into order has the best effect on newcomers. We cannot, however, judge by external order of the real effect of the presence of the casuals. Whatever evil they may have learnt during their vagrant life, they know that it is for their interest to submit to discipline while at school, to conceal what could bring them into disgrace with their superiors, and avoid conduct and language which would entail punishment. That such children are bad companions to others, who may not have had the misfortune to be exposed to the same bad influence, cannot be denied. Whatever discipline may exist in school, children in the playground and dormitories are under little supervision. In most of the schools, although the window of an officer's bedroom opens into the

dormitory, there is no one present to prevent conversation from the hour when the children go to bed
until the bedtime of the officer in charge. I think
it of great importance that some plan should be
adopted for the supervision of the dormitories during
these hours. The experience of those best qualified
to pronounce on the subject is, that such supervision
is absolutely necessary. In the play-yards the children are practically free to do as they please, for the
most active and conscientious yard-mistress could
not be within hearing of all the children, or know
what was going on at the other end of the play-grounds.
That children learn what is evil from each other is not
an imaginary danger. Several of the matrons and
mistresses have spoken to me on the subject.

. . . .

So far for the probable bad effects of the society
of casual children upon the others; but apart from
this it seems to me doubtful whether the present system acts favourably upon the casuals themselves.

Without here entering into the larger question of
whether the present system might not with advantage
be modified even for the children permanently at
school, there can be little doubt that shorter school
hours and far more labour in the open air would have
a beneficial effect both on the moral and physical
natures of children accustomed to a vagrant life.
The Secretary of the Red Hill Reformatory said that
not only did exercise in the fresh air improve the health

of the boys, but the cultivation of the earth raised them morally.

At Mettray and other such institutions the same facts have been recognised. If out-door labour does so much for the boys at Red Hill and elsewhere, why should not a similar system be tried for the casual children of workhouses, and with a few modifications, for the girls as well as the boys? The casuals being accustomed to out-door habits and much movement and liberty, must find the long school hours very irksome, and it would probably be more easy to interest them in out-door work than in books.

As to the objection that if the two classes of children were separated, no masters or mistresses would be found to undertake the management of the casual schools, it is true that the management of such schools would require talents of a particular kind; but no difficulty is found in getting teachers and mistresses for reformatory and industrial schools. . . .

.   .   .   .

There is a small class of girls now to be found in every pauper school, who seem to me out of place there. I mean those physically afflicted, *e.g.* scrofulous, and those whose sight is seriously affected.

The number of such children in each school is not large, but cases exist in every school. Matrons know that these girls never remain in service, even if people can be found to take them on trial. They are sure soon to be dismissed for stupidity, or physical incapacity.

No official likes to consign these poor girls to the adult ward of a workhouse, and thus, in practice, the rule that girls must not remain in school after the age of 16 is in their case frequently evaded. I have found girls of this class at the schools up to 18, or even beyond that age. The matron employs them in any work they are capable of doing about the establishment; but only a few can thus be provided for, and sooner or later they drift to the workhouse. And even while they are kept at school their position is unsatisfactory and sad.

I should recommend that girls unlikely on account of physical incapacity to be able to go to service, should be placed singly with families in the country. With a little trouble proper homes might be found for girls so afflicted, their keep would cost hardly more than in the workhouse, and they would be infinitely happier. The earlier the age at which the girls could be placed in such families the better, for their presence in the school is bad for their companions, and unprofitable to themselves, because they need more direct individual care than can be given them in a large school. But in a home such powers of usefulness as they possess would have more room for development, and through being useful to others their lives would become brighter.

.   .   .   .

The case of imbecile girls (not idiots, but mentally weak and incapable) is even more sad than that of the physically afflicted. Girls who are physically unhealthy or deficient can, to a certain extent, take care of themselves; but the imbeciles, who occasionally take their discharge from the workhouse, not being able to protect themselves, frequently become mothers of illegitimate children. . . .

.   .   .   .

At one of the large schools a separate block of new buildings has recently been set apart as an infant department. Here children up to five years of age are placed under the care of nurses, assisted by girls from the body of the school. From the nursery they pass into the infant school (still in the separate block), where girls remain till seven years old, and boys till ten.

I wish to call attention to these plans, the special features of which are the entire separation of the infants from the mass of the school, and the employment of elder girls in the care of the infants, because I would earnestly recommend their more general adoption.

If a certain number of the 16 metropolitan schools were by the consent of the different Boards of Guardians set apart as infant establishments, the plan would, I believe, be a gain in two ways, for such infant schools might be made excellent training places for girls for a year or two before going to service, and the separate establishments for the infants would allow of the system being more adapted to their physical needs

than is now practicable. Many, indeed one may
say most, of these pauper infants are of weakly constitution, and need more tending than stronger children
of the same age. They are consequently often apathetic, and it would be a great gain to have the
help of young girls who would take the place of "the
elder sister" in our own nurseries, in leading on the
little ones to lively play and exercise of various kinds.
Better arrangements might be made for their physical
improvement, and the number of older girls who
would be under training in the school, would make it
possible for each infant to have a little mother almost
to itself, who, under the direction of the nurse, would
attend to and amuse the child or children under her
care. Such training would be of great service to the
girls, who on going to place have often to look after
young children, and they would have gained some
knowledge which would stand them in good stead
if they married and became mothers.

I would have as little machinery as possible in these
infant establishments. The girls would do all the
house-work, as well as learn how to manage the
infants.

I should like that, on attaining 12 years, the girls
from the other schools should be sent for two years'
training in these infant establishments, before going to
place. If the number of girls was found to be too
great to make it possible to give them so long as two
years' training in these establishments, then they
would take their turn according to age, and possibly

some school be set apart for them from which they could, as vacancies arose, be drafted into the infant establishments. These infant establishments would be schools of domestic training fitted for teaching the girls the practical duties of life.

By 12 years old a girl in the metropolitan workhouse schools is generally able to read and write fairly, and do the first four rules of arithmetic; if she has been long in the school, her scholastic proficiency is far beyond this. When passed on to the infant establishments, an hour or two in school each day, would keep up the amount of knowledge already acquired, and allow time for training the general intelligence. Many of the superintendents and matrons agree with me as to the great advantage it would be to the girls to have more intelligent domestic training, and think that there is not at present sufficient time given to this object. If the girls on attaining 12 years, were sent to infant establishments, where the chief object would be to teach them to use their intelligence to fit them for being good servants, I believe it would be an excellent plan.

A girl is not necessarily a better woman because she knows the height of all the mountains of Europe, and can work out a fraction in her head; but she is decidedly better fitted for the duties she will be called upon to perform in life, if she knows how to wash and tend a child, cook simple food well, and thoroughly clean a house. To do these duties really well, needs not only intelligence, but special training.

I am very anxious that it should not be supposed that I advocate a low intellectual standard of teaching, either for paupers or other children, or that I have any sympathy with certain popular theories about the sufficiency of cooking and needlework for the complete development of the female understanding. I am on the other side altogether, but I think that in the case of these children, the amount of positive scholastic knowledge which they acquire, is not so important as the amount of intelligence which can be developed, and of household knowledge which can be imparted to them. I believe that, apart from the supreme necessity of improving their moral condition, their wits would be very much sharpened by a greater variety of occupation, more general reading, more amusement, and more cultivation of natural sympathy.

Hitherto I have spoken only of the gain in facilities for domestic training, and the development of general intelligence; but I would urge the plan of these infant establishments still more because of the moral gain to the girls.

One of the greatest objections to the plan of bringing up girls in large schools is, that they are unable to get the cherishing care and individual attention that is of far more importance in the formation of a girl's character than anything else in the world. It is the fault of no one in particular that at a large school a girl's affections are not called out. The officers have so much routine work to get through, that it is absolutely impossible for them to give sufficient time to individualising and influencing the girls under their care. The inquiries I have made on all sides have convinced me that what is wanted in the education of the girls is more *mothering*. Many of them who have fought their way bravely, and are doing well in life have indicated this to me. One will say, "We were kindly enough treated, but I felt very lonely"; another, "I was very fond of Miss A., but there were so many of us to look after that she could not be expected to make much of me." And so on.

If this is the opinion of girls who are successful in life, it would, I am sure, be echoed by those who have dropped out of sight, or done badly.

I would not only have separate schools for children under eight or nine years old, but I would break up the mass of children in these infant schools into groups, and return as far as possible to the natural order of families. I would have each nurse represent the head of a family, with a certain number of infants under her exclusive care, and a certain number of girls in training under her orders, who would help her with the children, and learn all sorts of house-work. If enormous wards had to be utilised I would consider whether they could not be partitioned into smaller rooms, so as to make one part the kitchen, another the day-room, and so on.

The schoolroom alone would be common to all the children, and this I should like to see managed on the same principle as German kindergartens, and the

best French salles d'asile. I would have shorter
school hours, constant change of occupation, much
gentle gymnastics, the companionship of the elder
girls in play, and from the tenderest years, a syste-
matic explanation and enforcement of the laws of
health.

.   .   .   .

Such a redistribution of the children as I have
suggested might require some change in the staff of
officers and servants employed in the schools; and
independently of any such alteration of plan, there
are two or three ways in which I think this staff might
be rendered more efficient.

The superintendent and matron are responsible
for working the whole machine of the school.

The schoolmaster and schoolmistress are secondary
in rank to them, so that with the exception of the
chaplain and doctor, who are heads of their own
departments, the superintendent and matron are
supposed to have absolute authority.

But the inferior officers and servants are appointed
not by them, but by the boards of management.   The
rate of wages, and in some cases even the question
of granting a holiday to a servant, have to be referred
to the School Committee. . . .

.   .   .   .

The trainers for the boys are almost always first-
rate workmen, and receive high wages.   In a school
where the girls' yard-mistress (whose duties resemble

those of the drill master who has charge of the boys)
received only 15£. yearly, the salary of the drill
master was 40£. a year. The few pounds more wages
necessary to secure a thoroughly competent servant,
who would have a good influence in every way over
the girls, would be well bestowed in fitting the girls
to keep their places. . . .

. . . .

I wish to also call attention to the fact that the
superintendents and matrons of these schools are in
numbers of cases very much overworked, and the
hardest workers and most conscientious, just those
in short who feel the strain, and need rest the most,
have at times felt their responsibility too deeply to
take a vacation at all.

I know of one matron who went away seven years
ago for a fortnight's vacation, but finding everything
out of gear on her return, has never been able to make
up her mind to take a holiday again. Another matron
has had two days' holiday in two years. A superintendent has not been absent from the establishment
a single night for two years, and during these two
years has had only one day out. I find again officers
who tell me that they are often obliged to attend to,
and post up their books on Sundays, having found it
impossible to get through their work during the week.

Considering the constant strain and anxiety that
must be felt by conscientious people in so responsible
a situation as these officers hold, I think it not only

wrong, but most unwise, that they should feel themselves unable to have even a fortnight's vacation in the year. If they could be *obliged* to take a holiday I think it would be found a good plan, both in their own interest and in that of the school.

The difficulty of breaking the monotony of the lives of the children in pauper schools, by giving regular vacations as in other schools, seems insurmountable. . . .

. . . They are in school (with the exception of those whose relatives have them out from time to time) all the year round and the only interruption of the daily school routine is the half holiday once, or (in some schools) twice a week, and the yearly or half-yearly treat.

These treats are so much looked forward to that they form points of departure for the dates of the year. Events are classed as "before or after the last visit to the Crystal Palace," &c.

Both boards of management and school officers organise these treats with great heartiness and goodwill. But it is a serious expense to send 800 or 1,000 children for a day's pleasuring, and one that could not be often repeated in the year. A friend of mine who lives near one of the schools, offered to take some of the girls to the Crystal Palace, paying of course all expenses. Her offer was refused. It was not in the power of the superintendent to give the necessary permission.

I wish that the Guardians would authorise super-

intendents to allow persons of discretion to take some
of the children for a day's outing from time to time.
Such treats might prove strong incentives to good
conduct, and under the care of a trustworthy intelligent person would be of great use to the children.
In a country excursion they might have their attention
called to natural objects, the habits of birds and
animals, the names and uses of plants, trees, &c.
I think such glimpses of the world beyond the school
walls, would tend to brighten the children, and to
dissipate the lethargy and dullness which is often
noticed and lamented by the officers of the schools, in
children of this class.

A. II. Sanitary Conditions.

It was my duty to examine closely the sanitary
arrangements of these Institutions, as being a most
important part of the system under which pauper
children are brought up; and I did so all the more
diligently, from having been struck from the first with
signs of what appeared to me a low physical condition
among them; round shoulders, narrow chests, and
frames of stunted growth met the eye more frequently
than could be accounted for by the pauper origin and
habits of the children. There were, besides, shorn
heads and weak eyes, speaking of recent ophthalmia
and ringworm. I afterwards learnt that cases of near
and defective sight are of frequent occurrence, though
the authorities attribute these ailments, in most
cases, to the effects of ophthalmia.

I will give my observations upon sanitary matters, under the four heads of—

1. Schoolroom arrangements.
2. Dormitory arrangements.
3. Food.
4. Exercise and play.

1. *Schoolroom arrangements:*

There is no difficulty in accounting for the round shoulders and narrow chests of young children who have to sit three hours at a time at lessons, on forms not fitted with backs, and obliged to seek relief by contorted attitudes which it is painful to watch. These observations do not, however, apply in full to all the schools, as in some cases the three hours' lessons are broken by ten minutes' run.

Still it is rare to see backs fitted to the forms, while in some schoolrooms the position of the bench with regard to the desk, is such as to make it impossible for the children to write without some contortion of the figure. Add to this, that in many instances the desks are so placed that the children face the light during lessons, than which nothing can be worse for the eyes. The observance of a few simple rules in the arrangement of the schoolroom would set all this right, and in my opinion would greatly conduce to the health of the children. I often found the schoolrooms cold, and yet perceptibly close and oppressive from want of thorough ventilation.

This remark applies with much greater force to:—

2. *Dormitory arrangements:*

With doors and windows wide open, and the rooms empty, I found in several cases a bad close smell. I had but to imagine what it could be after a night of overcrowding. On one occasion I went through the dormitories of a school at 5.30 A.M., and it needed no doctor to tell me that the children sleeping there had been breathing poison. . . .

. . . I always found doors and windows set well open during the day. The officers often owned with sorrow, that notwithstanding every care in these respects, the rooms "smelt very bad" after the children had been for a few hours in bed, and that they knew the rooms were "too crowded."

But what can subordinates do if their masters think foul air innocuous? A matron of long experience, whose opinion (corroborated by that of her husband) ought to have had weight, told me that there were too many children for the size of the dormitory, and that the doctor had told her that the air was most impure by the time the night was over. On the unwholesomeness of the crowded room being represented to the Guardians, the complaint was not regarded as well-founded; but on the contrary, an opinion was expressed that more beds might be put into the room.

I wish it could be provided that (besides 50 square feet of superficial area for each bed) an arrangement should be made, by which there should always be thorough ventilation into the open air; and supplementary to this, a ventilating apparatus that could be regulated according to change of season or temperature.

. . . .

. . . Considering the importance of this question of pure air, I much wish that a professional inquiry might be made, as to the necessary means to be taken to *secure* efficient ventilation of dormitories and school-rooms.

Of course if the ventilation were increased, the children would need more blankets on their beds, and possibly a somewhat different diet; but the increased expenditure would be well bestowed.

But insufficient ventilation and overcrowding are not the only deleterious influences to be found in the dormitories.

In some of them, gas is burned day and night, for the sake of warmth. In others, open vessels are used during the night. In all the dormitories I observed that the clothing worn by the children during the day, was left in the room. I think these three causes of impure air might without much difficulty be removed.

It would be a far better plan to warm the dormitories by fires rather than by gas. . . .

With regard to the second deleterious influence, I should propose that where utensils are used in the dormitories, they should in all cases be provided with covers.

I think it a very necessary part of the training of a girl in housework, that she should learn the necessity of proper care in the cleaning of chamber utensils; and I would not, if only on this account, have water-closets in all cases substituted for them; but it is quite possible, and absolutely necessary, by the use of covers to prevent the evils of unwholesome effluvia.

With regard to the children's clothes being left in the room at night. Of course the rules as to the change of linen, greatly affect the degree in which the clothes worn by day will vitiate the air of the room in which they are left at night.

I found that, as a rule, in all the schools, only the infants are provided with nightgowns. The girls wear their day shift at night, and wear one shift, day and night, for a week. Those who wear flannel, wear their flannel shift, day and night, for a fortnight. In schools where the day dresses are made of the same woollen material for both winter and summer, all the girls, and especially the hard workers, must have their clothes, throughout the summer, saturated with perspiration.

When the state of the girls' under garments is contrasted with the often spotless purity of the pinafores in which they appear in the schoolroom, and with the perfectly white counterpanes on their beds, I cannot but think it a sad example of "cleansing the outside of the cup and platter" only.

At some of the schools a little basket is placed at the foot of each bed, into which the child puts her

clothes at night, carefully folded. At other schools
the clothes are placed on the bed, and in cold weather
they are undoubtedly of use, for they help to keep
the children warm in bed; but it would be a better
plan to add a blanket or rug to the covering of each
bed, than to leave these dirty garments in the dormitories during the night.

In some of the schools the boots are put at night
in pigeon-holes outside the dormitories; a capital plan,
and one that I should be glad to see adopted for the
clothing in general.

.   .   .   .

3. *As to food:*

The food seemed generally of good quality, sufficient in quantity, and on the whole tolerably well
cooked; but variety is not sufficiently studied, and
the food provided is not always relished by the children; and simply on that account cannot properly
nourish them.

It is said, by those who think they see insurmountable difficulties in the way of bringing in a variation
of ·diet, that the children of the London poor get
none; but only ring the changes on bread and butter,
red herrings, cockles, hot potatoes, and sugar plums.
But I know that tripe, and cow heel, and sausages,
and occasional rashers of bacon come in to vary the
cockles and red herrings; nor must it be forgotten
that when there is a glut in the market of any vegetable or fruit, costermongers are found selling the

contents of their barrows in the very poorest parts of London. The street children thus get apples and pears, radishes, and lettuce, currants and blackberries; even penny slices of pineapple are occasionally within their reach.

The opinion of those who have studied the subject, is distinctly in favour of the necessity of a varied diet. The children in these schools get a great deal more meat than in their own poor homes, but they have little or no green vegetable, no fruit, and, as a rule, very little sugar; all of which things ought to be found in the dietary of children. An occasional dinner of bread and cheese and onion, or bread and fat bacon, would be inexpensive, easily prepared, and much enjoyed; and when apples were cheap, an apple might be substituted for an onion. I think that fruit and different kinds of vegetables should find their way into the schools, not as a treat to the children, but as articles of food necessary for keeping the children in health. . . .

In some of the schools good arrangements are now made for insuring that the children get their dinners hot; but at others it is the habit to serve out the dinner, and put each portion on the plate before the children come in to the dining hall. The grace before meals too is often long, and is generally made still longer by being sung instead of said, a custom which I think might be dispensed with, to the advantage of the children.

I have talked on these matters with servants who had been brought up in Union schools, and found them all agreed on the diet question. Some of them have added that on soup days they had often gone from breakfast to supper with only the bit of bread allowed with the soup at dinner; and that they rarely eat all their dinner on meat days, because it had got cold before they went in to dinner, and the tepid fat made them sick.

.   .   .   .

4. *Exercise and play:*

The direct development of the bodily powers by means of exercise, and the time spent in the play-ground, is a subject which I regard as being in importance second only to that of food.

In this respect I could not but admire the provision made for the boys, by means of a regular drill, and the cultivation of band music. It seems a pity that in all the schools, as is the case now in one, girls should not be drilled as well as boys. It would be a great advantage to them, both as to health and appearance. But if they are to be drilled, a change in their dress would be necessary. They could not do extension exercises in the tight-fitting, and often ill-cut bodices which they now wear. It would be impossible in these establishments, where so much work has to be got through, to cut out and carefully fit the bodice of each girl to her figure; but it would not be difficult to devise a loose jacket or bodice, that would be kept tidily in its place by a waistband, except when the free use of the arms was required. I think such loose jackets would be more wholesome for growing girls than the present style of dress, and they certainly would be able to do their industrial work more easily in such a bodice than in a tight-fitting frock.

It cannot be denied that more is done in these schools for the physical improvement of the boys than of the girls. In very few of the schools are the girls drilled, in none of them are the girls taught to swim. In all the large schools I find a good swimming bath, and am told that the boys greatly enjoy the exercise. I cannot see why the girls should not share an advantage already provided for the boys; a matter easily arranged by a special appropriation of the swimming bath to the girls, on certain hours or days. The yard or drill mistress might be required to learn herself, and to teach swimming to the girls.

It appeared to me that with some striking exceptions, the girls at these schools showed a curious dulness as to play, which is significant of undeveloped natures. On making this remark to some of the officers, I found it was a matter of common observation. I have seldom seen energetic play going on, either in the play-grounds or day-rooms. Though there is a marked superiority in this point in some schools over others, I have rarely found, when I have asked the girls to show me a game, that they could set themselves spontaneously to anything of the sort; all seemed to depend on the promptings of the yard

mistress. There appears to be no tradition of games
in the schools. To teach them to play with intelligence and enjoyment, would be well worth the trouble,
as an educational process. Playing with energy
would be a step towards working with energy.

So far on the four points of sanitary arrangements.
My observations may seem minute, but as all these
little things go to build up or to deteriorate, to
strengthen or weaken the physical fabric of each
pauper child, we cannot attach too much importance
to such details. Unless we strengthen and develop
the bodies of these children by every possible means,
we shall endeavour in vain to raise them in the social
scale. If they go out to the fight of life with weakly
bodies, they cannot long be self-supporting. They
will be sickly and helpless themselves, and become
the parents of still more sickly and helpless children.
It must be ever remembered that the great temptation of all is drink, and that a low physical condition,
more than anything else, gives strength to this temptation.

.   .   .   .

I must not dismiss the subject of sanitary conditions
without a word about the infirmaries.

I was generally struck with an air of comfort and
order which prevailed in them, and I know how difficult it would be to make any important change in
their management.

Yet I strongly feel that something more ought to
be done for the large number of children who must

pass a considerable part of their time in what, at the best, must be called a dismal confinement.

I do not mean that the buildings are in themselves dismal, but that the life the children lead while in hospital, is beyond expression dreary.

. . . .

Even an hour's reading aloud to the children, putting new ideas into their minds, and giving them something to talk about, would be a great benefit; an occasional singing lesson, and materials for knitting or netting, might also be of great use in getting them safely through the time in hospital.

I believe that there are many ladies who would be glad to give an hour or two regularly to some of those purposes, if the way were not closed, as at present it is. It is believed by the school authorities that if ladies were allowed the run of the infirmaries, difficulties might arise in enforcing necessary discipline, and that there would be antagonism between the lady visitors, and the hospital authorities.

I think that any possibility of this apprehended interference would be avoided, by arranging that a ward or two should be set apart, and called convalescent wards, to which lady visitors might have free access on certain days, and at fixed hours.

. . . .

At the great Children's Hospital at Paris, employment is enforced; and gymnastics and singing classes, under professors, are considered quite as much a part of the treatment as bathing or medicine.

The question of the possibility of having the sick children from each school placed in special hospitals, instead of following the present plan of annexing an infirmary to each school, has been not unfrequently discussed.

Such an arrangement would have great advantages, in my opinion, over the present system.

I may as well mention here, that there is an idea among some of the officials, that children will occasionally make themselves ill, for the sake of getting into the infirmary. I do not myself believe this, and I am glad to say, that I have found it denied more often than it is asserted.

But if it were true, it seems to me that it would be an argument for introducing something like lessons and employment into the hospitals, so that the "great attraction of entire idleness," of which I hear so much, and believe so little, might be removed.

It is indeed distressing to any one who cares for children, to think of all the time and opportunities lost in the stagnant infirmary life. Surely it is a pity not to let in some of the immense quantity of outside love and benevolence, to enliven the present dreary state of things.

A. III. Moral and Industrial Training.

. . . .

A little child growing up in a home, is receiving constant education through a set of motives which, as much as possible, should be called into play, even in school life. She sits on the door step and is trusted to take care of baby at a very early age; or she is sent on an errand, or set to perform some small domestic duty.

These little incidents of cottage life, contain the germ of all valuable qualities; affection, ambition, sense of usefulness, sense of responsibility, sense of membership, presence of mind.

Then, too, in a cottage home, a child gets the education that comes through the pressure of actual need. She knows the comfort of rewarded industry, and has the proud delight of helping mother, and the prospect of one day doing for herself, and helping the family.

Much of all this is of course unattainable under the circumstances of school life, but I venture to think that it is not altogether so.

There is no influence more softening than the care of little children; every mother knows how soon her own little girl develops the maternal instinct, and how good a thing it is to cultivate it. And this is an instinct that may be developed even at school. At one of the metropolitan schools, where the female influence was strong and good, I noticed that the hair of several of the tiny children was unusually well tended, and even in some instances curled, and the little faces exceedingly clean and polished. I was told that, as a reward, the best girls were allowed to be little mothers to some child whom they tended and watched over, and these specially bright children were those who had a little mother to see to them. I was shown letters from girls in service, and saw that the special affection of the girl for the child she had nursed, continued long after she left school. There were constant mentions of little Sally or Polly, (the child who had been under her special care).

. . . .

It is more difficult to see how, in a school, girls can learn anything of the value of money or of the cost of what they wear. A lady of large experience told me that the difference in this point between girls from workhouse schools, and girls who had been brought up at home, was very remarkable. The workhouse school girls took no care of their clothes. The children had no experience of what clothes cost, had never denied themselves, nor seen any one else suffer privation, in order that they might have a new frock, or pair of boots. She has known them cut up their stockings and clothes, and hide the pieces in the dusthole, to avoid having the trouble of mending them, saying, "We shall have new ones given us."

If a child realises the difficulty of saving money for the purchase of some article of clothing, the moral effect is great. The same lady speaking on this subject, told me of an orphan girl, whose mother, a widow, had had a hard struggle to keep herself and child. This lady gave the child a pair of new boots, and noticed that she did not run about, or skip with the girls with whom she associated, as had been her wont.

On being questioned, the child said that "mother had taught her not to run about much when she got a pair of new boots, for fear of wearing them out too soon."

The ignorance of the cost of clothes, and the consequent carelessness about keeping them tidily mended, is repeatedly complained of by the mistresses of girls. I have found cases where they have cut up new straw bonnets, that had been provided for their outfit. This may be because they dislike to wear what they think a workhouse badge. But this excuse does not apply to the carelessness often shown about keeping their clothes and stockings mended.

Owing to ignorance of the value of money, and the art of purchasing materials of clothing, the girls are liable to be imposed upon, and mistresses have been known to make them take worthless old clothes instead of their wages. A very intelligent girl, who had been in place for some years, told me that she had not yet learnt to distinguish between a good serviceable material for a dress, and a comparatively worthless one; and that she always tried to secure the assistance of a friend in making her choice.

If infant establishments, such as I have elsewhere proposed, could be used as training schools for girls after 12 years of age, I think many more of the good educational influences of family life might be introduced. The matrons of such establishments might be authorised to allow persons of discretion, known and approved of by the Boards of Management, to take the girls in turn, out occasionally, to show them something of practical life outside the school. "Shopping" would doubtless form part of the interest of the day's outing, and would afford opportunity for some little observation and experience of the ways of the outward world.

I heard very common complaints of the sullen tempers, apathy of manner, and violent passion, of girls who were doing fairly well in place. The same faults appear in a greatly heightened degree, in girls who turn out badly in after life.

The governor of a large prison, from which I got a return of the number of girls educated at workhouse schools now in that prison, writes that "girls brought up at pauper schools are the worst prisoners *by far* of any that come under his care." . . .

From numbers of refuges and homes, at which I have made inquiries, I hear the same thing. "Very bad tempers, apathetic, untruthful." Testimony to the same effect is given me by ladies who have large experience of friendless and fallen girls. They assure me that they can almost always tell a workhouse school girl before inquiring where she was educated. They say that the girls have a hardness about them which it is most difficult to break down, and are less amenable to authority than the other inmates of the homes. They add, that if a girl can be convinced that she is individually cared for, and that her misconduct causes real sorrow to the matron or lady who has had to do with her, she becomes a different creature. . . .

It would be a great incentive to exertion, and might lead the girls to take more interest in their work, if they could earn money by increased exertion. At Reformatory schools, the girls receive a sum of money weekly, as a small percentage on the industrial work they perform. Part of this is put into the saving's bank for them when they leave, and part of it they are allowed to spend. But as it is illegal for a pauper to earn money, no payment for industrial work can be made to girls at these schools. Not only would it be illegal to appropriate any portion of the Poor rate to this object, but if the necessary funds for rewarding a girl by letting her earn some money, were provided by private benevolence, the money could not legally be bestowed on her.

Nor could she earn anything by the cultivation of a garden during play hours, (a plan that has succeeded so well at the Paxton and Eyemouth schools) for all the school land is supposed to be under cultivation for the lessening of the Rates, and the instruction of the boys. Yet it would be a great stimulus to exertion if a girl could have the pleasure of earning money, and as an educational process it should not be neglected.

.   .   .   .

... A hearty laugh is a great help to growth and health. The monotony of life in a large school is a great evil, and everything that can break it is to be welcomed.

Those who have observed the transformation worked upon the usually dull and apathetic countenances of these children, on the occasions of their annual or half-yearly treats, or even by a chance word of kindly interest, will not doubt the benefit which would arise from allowing the sympathy and goodwill of the governesses and matrons to show itself in contriving little surprises, and variations in the school routine. It would not be difficult for those who have their hearts in the matter to do this, since a mere *change* of order and employment, if introduced as a pleasant thing, is sure to be considered such by children.

At one of the large schools the superintendent, on his own responsibility, gives the children repeated half holidays during the summer, with the best effect. Of course it depends on the amount of liberty given to the superintendent, whether he can do this or not, but it certainly is the best thing possible for the children.

The amount of actual knowledge imparted should, I think, be a secondary consideration. Some of the time which is now spent in mere learning, might be more profitably given to play and exercise, in teaching children to enjoy innocent pleasures, in cultivating their intelligence, and teaching them to think about and understand common things. The dulness of a life which is only kept by force from open wrong-doing must be very oppressive, and a child who has had little habitual enjoyment, is very likely to "break out," and have anything but innocent "larks and sprees," as soon as school life is over.

I see an indication of this in the fact that children from these schools are unusually fond of smart dress. I have been told by mistresses of these girls, that "Hannah would always wear a red bow in her cap, even at her dirty work," and that, "Sarah had a craving for shining beads." One mistress said, that "Mary Anne was a very good girl, but she *would* wear a white satin bonnet with a yellow flower in it, though she told the child that it was not respectable to go out on Sunday bedizened like that." I know a whole family of children who had passed some years at one of the pauper schools, who could not be kept from stealing the shining buckles, and bright pretty things belonging to their schoolfellows, in the day school to which they went, on coming out of the workhouse school. They did not seem to understand that it was wrong, and found it at all events an irresistible temptation to take possession of the first pretty thing they saw. I hear of girls in service, not bad in other ways, who pilfered beads, or bright ribbons.

I should like to ornament the walls of the schools, and the dormitories and passages, with paintings, and scrolls, and illuminations, and texts, and bits of poetry, all in bright colours; the children would learn the texts and the poetry almost unconsciously, and the colours would be a delight; and I should like them to be made to keep themselves warm in winter by good active games.

In the large playrooms there are great capabilities

for fun.   Room for dancing Sir Roger de Coverley and country dances, and for keeping off chilblains by exercise.   There is a capital game, a sort of Montagne Russe, that might be managed at almost every school; a great smoothly-planed board, placed against a rail or block of wood, at rather a steep incline.   Children will amuse themselves with this by the hour, and get all sorts of gymnastics and fun out of it.

And in summer, I wish that the love of cultivating gardens could be encouraged, by giving a little plot of ground, not under cultivation for the lessening of the rates, to some of the elder children, and that they should be stimulated to industry by school flower shows, &c. . . .

Much fun and exercise might be got out of a cart such as is used at the College for the blind, at Norwood.   There are two seats in the cart, and the children take it in turns to be in the carriage, or in the shafts, and there is endless amusement in taking drives with a good team.

Among other plans for stimulating the interest of girls in work, I would suggest that materials for different kinds of work might be given as prizes.   One girl who had learnt a new stitch, would teach another, and so hands and heads would be busy and interested. At one school I was told by the matron, that the children in the infirmary had carefully picked out the red wool with which the blankets were overcast, and by straightening hair-pins had formed knitting needles, and taught themselves to knit up wool. . . .

    •   •   •   •   •   •   •   •   •

One most important branch of education is entirely
neglected in these, as in almost all other schools.
Children, as a rule, are taught nothing about the laws of
health; yet all children are curious and eager to hear
any facts about familiar things; and it would be easy
to instruct them in the "why" and "because" of the
duties which a knowledge of these laws lays upon
everyone. If physiology, and some sound knowledge
of natural laws were insisted on, as part of the education at these schools, it would be necessary that the
teachers and officers should not themselves be ignorant
on these subjects. It is the ignorance under which
young people grow up, of the consequences which
God has attached to the neglect of certain simple
rules concerning the care of the body, which, more
than any other single cause, leads to reckless habits,
equally injurious to mental and bodily health.

The deleterious effect of excess of every kind, of
breathing impure air, of impeded circulation, together
with the importance of personal cleanliness, and other
such matters, should be impressed upon children in
every possible way. . . .

So little attention has hitherto been paid in ele-
mentary education to these subjects, that the teachers
themselves would require to be taught. It is certain
that a great part of the difficulty which is found in
maintaining good sanitary conditions in these schools,
proceeds from the ignorance of the grown-up people,
servants, and others, on whose care the various arrangements for securing ventilation and cleanliness
depend. . . .

If the officers understood why it was bad for themselves, as well as for the children, to live in unhealthy conditions, they would be more energetic in attending to sanitary regulations, and would work heartily and intelligently with the doctor and matron.

.   .   .   .

On board the "Goliath," the head boy of each mess is responsible for the cleanliness of table, knives, mugs, &c. By enforcing, and setting the example of the strictest cleanliness, he can earn a cake for his mess. It would be possible to adopt some such plan at these schools; and a sense of responsibility might be awakened in the girls, by trusting them with some particular piece of work, the due performance of which might be acknowledged by a treat of some kind.

To excite a real interest in needlework, it would be a good plan to have a few large dolls for the girls to dress. Contriving and cutting out suits of clothes for these dolls in play hours, would help the girls more than anything else could do, to understand how to cut out their own clothes.

All children ought by some means to be made bright, self dependent, and capable of innocent enjoyment; and I do not see any other means but those I propose, by which these ends are likely to be attained. Those who know how to enjoy themselves thoroughly, are always the best workers.

Having discovered, at the outset of my inquiry, that in a school I was visiting, caning girls was re-

peatedly practised, I was led to make special inquiries on the subject of corporal punishment of girls
in the metropolitan schools, and have come to the
conclusion that the punishment has a demoralising
effect. The practice seems to be on the decline. . . .

B. IN THE WORLD.

.   .   .   .   .

B. I. CHOICE OF SITUATIONS.

.   .   .   .

As I have said, it is at present the rule that the Relieving Officer shall visit, and report to the Guardians,
on the places of service to which the girls are sent;
so that practically, the decision rests with him. It
is supposed that the Relieving Officer will, from his
intimate knowledge of the districts in which his other
work lies, be able, better than anyone else, to ascertain whether the people applying for a servant are
respectable and solvent persons, who bear a good
character in the neighbourhood. So far as this he may
perhaps be able to ascertain; though not a few instances have come to my knowledge, in which I feel
convinced that the people with whom the girls have
been placed, were not even in outward circumstances
fit to be trusted with a servant. But a place may be
an altogether unfit one for a girl, although the Relieving Officer may have been rightly satisfied on the
score of outward respectability. The low rate of

wages given to these girls, and the excellent outfit with which they are provided, makes them sought after by many people who, a few years ago, would have done their own house work, whose income does not permit them to keep a superior servant, and who often look on their little servant as a mere drudge.

As a matter of fact, I have sometimes found girls placed in very unsuitable situations, *e.g.*, in neighbourhoods so low that, in one case, a lady was told that none but mission women would venture there; or as single servant where the work was quite beyond their physical powers. There is also more common neglect of obvious precautions, such as not putting girls out in neighbourhoods where they will be thrown in the way of bad relations, or placing them near barracks, or in any disreputable districts.

If there were any difficulty in finding situations for these children, there might be something to be said for taking any places that were offered, without so rigid an inquiry as to their merits. But I am told by every matron without exception, that the applications at the schools for servants are far beyond the supply of girls ready to go out; and that they could place three times as many girls as there are of an age to go to service.

I cannot approve of the inspection and choice of places being committed to men; though with regard to general respectability and solvency, use may no doubt be made of the information possessed by the Relieving Officer.

It requires the eye of a motherly woman to perceive the small details which go to render a situation desirable or otherwise for a young girl. At present, in a few of the schools, the matron or one of female under officers, is sent to see the mistress applying for a servant, and to ascertain whether the place is a fit one. This system is attended by very satisfactory results. The situations in which I found these girls were, it appeared to me, more suitable than those chosen by Relieving Officers, and the girls themselves were as a rule doing better.

B. II. SUPERVISION.

. . . .

No uniform plan is adopted for the supervision of girls in service, nor any sufficient provision made for this duty.

At some of the schools the chaplain undertakes to visit them. In others, it is the joint duty of chaplain and relieving officer, or of matron and relieving officer.

. . . .

Much is, I am sure, done for the effectual supervision of the girls when the duty of visiting is in the hands either of chaplains or matrons. If the visiting even in such cases is imperfect, it is the fault of the system and not of the individuals. But I hope that my kind allies, the chaplains, will forgive me for expressing my belief that, valuable as their services are in visiting the girls, the work would be still more effectually done by a woman. There are many questions arising between a girl and her mistress that would never be laid before a man, and many little troubles occur in a girl's life that she would find it impossible to state to a man, no matter how long she had known him, nor how kind he might be. And this holds more especially in any matter of health, which is a question of the deepest importance to these girls, who have to support themselves by hard work. In schools where the supervision of girls in place is undertaken by the matron, I find the same good results from the arrangement, as are obtained by allowing her to have the selection of places. Considering, however, the extremely hard work and multifarious duties of the matron, such a plan, however successful in certain cases, could not be proposed for general adoption.

· · · · · · · · ·

B. III. GUARDIANSHIP.

As soon as a girl is placed out in service, she becomes legally her own mistress, and may dispose of herself as she chooses. It is true that some years ago, in consequence of a case of gross ill-usage of a workhouse girl in place, an Act was passed (a clause of which I have quoted elsewhere) providing that the relieving officer should visit girls up to the age of 16. But when a girl leaves her first situation, no matter how young she may be, even this small amount of legal protection ceases.

Nor have the Guardians power to protect the pauper children of the schools even until they are old enough to earn their own living, as I have mentioned in an earlier chapter of this report. Existing regulations require that the child shall, in all cases, accompany the parent, as often as the latter takes his discharge from the workhouse.

It thus happens that the children whom I have called casuals, are sometimes taken away from school as many as six times in the course of a year; during these absences there is frequently a relapse into bad habits, and in many cases the children are exposed to the most corrupting influences.

.   .   .   .

It can, however, be no economy of public money, to insist on the children of a reckless and vagrant parent following in his steps; on the contrary, such a course must entail a far heavier burden on the nation in the time to come.

I should like to see the provisions of the Industrial Schools Act, 1866 (29 & 30 Vict. c. 118), extended, so that the magistrates, or proper authority, might have power to order the detention of pauper children at school.

.   .   .   .

And here I venture to make a suggestion, which, knowing the tenderness of the English law with regard to the liberty of the subject (a tenderness with which I fully sympathise) I put forward with some hesitation.

The tendency of such a plan as I have just proposed would be, it will be alleged, to offer a premium to parents whose habits make them least sensible of their responsibility towards their children, to divest themselves of an unpleasant burden. To meet such an objection, I venture to propose that the principle of the law (34 & 35 Vict. c. 108) by which vagrants are, under certain circumstances, detainable in unions, be extended, and its provisions made applicable to all vagrant parents, *i.e.*, to those who have entered and discharged themselves (say) three times in one year. We must face the fact that there is a class of persons in existence who are determined to make a livelihood out of that which was intended to be a provision only in cases of unavoidable destitution. These persons ought, I think, not only to be detained for a short time, like the casual paupers mentioned in the Act, but set to work in separate workhouses at least till they had repaid their maintenance.

There are acres of half-cultivated and unreclaimed land where these paupers, segregated from the influences which have created in them a vicious temperament, might learn the blessing of work, and be returned to society as useful members. Let such an institution be set on foot in the Yorkshire moors, where the agricultural produce would find a ready market in the neighbouring manufacturing towns, and the first outlay would soon be repaid, and the annual expenditure provided for, and let the children of paupers detained in such an institution be kept at school close by, to

develope, in a pure atmosphere, some of the physical
strength without which they are too likely to tread
in their parent's footsteps.

.   .   .   .

This question of guardianship presents itself again,
under a slightly different aspect, when the children
are old enough to be self supporting, and are placed
in situations. . . .

I do not see why it should be impossible to extend
some protection to the children of paupers for a few
years after they leave school; say to the age of 18 or
20; and for this purpose, to confer on Boards of
Guardians a legal guardianship over those who, for a
limited time, say for five or seven years, have been
inmates of a pauper school. . . .

.   .   .   .

B. IV. PROTECTION WHEN OUT OF PLACE.

The importance of a girl's keeping her first place is
the greater, on account of the difficulty of providing
suitable protection for her when she is out of place. . . .

.   .   .   .

It was very startling to find the number of girls who
have failed in service and disappeared from view;
all the more knowing as we do what, in the case of
workhouse girls, "failure in service" generally means.

.   .   .   .

A plan has been suggested to me for calling forth the resources of volunteer benevolence on behalf of workhouse girls, which has already been tested by actual experience, in the case both of workhouse and other friendless girls, and which might meet the needs of the Metropolitan workhouse girls, if private efforts can be rendered permanently effective, by official aid and sanction.

The scheme proposes, that the charge of the girls when ready for service, shall be transferred from the different Unions to which they belong, to a central authority; and that a woman properly qualified shall be officially employed in choosing situations, and in visiting girls in place, as is now done by chaplain or relieving officer; and that in connexion with this official visitation, ladies shall be asked to aid in the supervision of the girls, and in encouraging them to do well by little plans formed in their own neighbourhood, and worked by themselves. Both the official visitors and the volunteer ladies, shall make regular reports of the girls under their charge. These reports shall be received at a central office, which shall include, under the same roof, a home for the protection of girls temporarily out of place, and a registry for young servants under the age of 18.

This scheme will be found fully drawn out in Appendix H.

CONCLUSION.

It will already have appeared from what I have written of my visits to pauper schools, that I was unfavourably impressed with the effect of thus massing children together in large numbers.

. . . I wished to ascertain whether, under other conditions, children of the same class appeared to prosper better.

I set out on a tour of inspection in some districts in England and Scotland where the system of boarding-out in families is adopted. . . .

I received the same impression everywhere, in favour of the free and natural mode of life afforded by cottage homes. . . .

.   .   .   .

[Here follows a recapitulation of the arguments in favour of boarding-out already given in her letter to *The Times.*]

The whole Poor Law system is a necessary evil, and I believe that the time will come when its provisions will be no longer necessary, when education, and improved social arrangements, will have triumphed over pauperism. The enormous buildings that are erected for the reception of pauper children, seem to point to a belief that we are to have an ever-increasing race of paupers throughout the centuries to come. Against such a belief boarding-out is a protest.

.   .   .   .

At the outset of my work I fully expected that the
result of my inquiries would show in favour of the
girls educated in the splendid district schools, where
no expense is spared, as compared with girls sent out
from the separate schools, which are often very in-
complete in their arrangements.   To my astonishment
the contrary appears to be the case.   (See Appendix F.)

This fact seems to me to show that, however carefully elaborated a system may be, under which girls
are brought together in large numbers, it will issue in
failure.

Thus I am forced to believe that the system of
large schools is not a good one for girls, and that
where it is not possible to place a girl in a family, she
should be brought up in a small school, where individual influence can be brought to bear on her.

The plan for the education of pauper children that
I should like to see adopted, would be that the orphan
children should be boarded out in cottage homes.

In the next place I should wish to break up the present schools, and to educate the deserted children
apart from the casual children.

For both classes of children I would adopt schools
of a more homelike character, arranged on the Mettray system, each house containing not more than
from 20 to 30 children of all ages.

Should this be pronounced impossible for the present, I would recur to the plan explained in a former
chapter, under the heading "Classification," of using
some of the existing schools as infant establishments,

in which girls after 12 years of age should receive special training; and I would re-class the remaining schools, using some as hospitals, and the others as schools for boys and girls.

The boys and girls schools I should like to divide into two classes. In one set of schools, permanent inmates only should be received, in the other casuals only; so that the special system of training which I wish to see adopted for the casual children, might be carried on in establishments exclusively devoted to this purpose.

I have, &c.

JANE ELIZABETH SENIOR.

To THE RIGHT HON. JAMES STANSFELD,
PRESIDENT OF THE LOCAL GOVERNMENT BOARD.

APPENDIX A.

BOARDED–OUT CHILDREN.

I went first to see the children boarded-out from Wrexham.

These children are boarded-out within their own union at the will of the guardians, not according to the boarding-out order issued by the Local Government Board. There is no boarding-out committee to look after the children, and it is in fact a species of out-door relief. I saw about 30 children boarded-out by the Wrexham guardians; some in the village school, others at the houses of their foster parents. In some of the houses the accommodation was insufficient, and hygienic conditions were not satisfactory, but the children seemed to me larger and more healthy looking than those in the metropolitan schools. I do not consider Wrexham a fair specimen of the boarding-out system. The Local Government Board order as to boarding-out not being adopted in this union, there is no committee to act under the Board of Guardians, and consequently there is no regular system of supervision.

Whether for this or for some other cause the experiment does not appear to have proved successful, as the Wrexham guardians have expressed their intention not to board-out any more children on account of several failures which have arisen among those boarded-out in April, 1871.

From Wrexham I went to Westmorland to see some of the pauper children from Bethnal Green, who are boarded-out at Burnside, Windermere, Ambleside, Troutbeck, and Grassmere. In this district I saw seventeen children.

The boarding-out in the Lake District is managed according to the boarding-out order of the Local Government Board. There is a committee of ladies, who undertake the supervision of the children, are careful in choosing proper homes for the little ones, and visit them constantly. Nothing can be more satisfactory than the state of the children, both morally and physically, though they come from one of the lowest parts of London. Miss Preusser (lady president of the boarding-out committee) says that the children when they arrived were weakly in body and dull, with little animal spirits, but that they soon began to improve in all ways. As a proof of what a change pure air and healthy conditions can make in children in one year, Miss Preusser told me that one little girl increased 16 lbs. in weight in the first year after her arrival from London, and her sister 12 lbs. in the same time. Another child I saw had grown more than a head in the year.

One very remarkable difference between the children in these homes and the children at the metropolitan pauper schools is their greater brightness and trustfulness of manner, and their readiness to answer questions, and tell one all about themselves and what they are doing.

.   .   .   .

From Cumberland I went to Edinburgh, where with Mr. Greig, inspector, and Mr. Cowan, one of the sub-inspectors of poor for the city parish, Edinburgh, I visited 63 children boarded-out from this parish. The inspection of the children and lunatics who are boarded-out is Mr. Cowan's constant and sole work; in other words, there is a special officer appointed to discharge this duty. Great importance is attached to the existence of such an officer, and a strong feeling prevails in Scotland that the work cannot be done by amateurs. A committee of the parochial board make once or twice a year a visit of inspection of the children boarded-out.

I found 22 of these children in villages about six miles out of Edinburgh, in the families of miners, and labourers on farms or the railroad. The houses are clean, most of them remarkably so; and the foster mothers turned down the beds, and showed the cleanliness of the bedding with great pride. We sought out the children at the different parish schools, as our visits to the homes were made during school hours. The pauper children looked quite as healthy as the others, and as their dress is purchased and arranged by their foster mothers, there is no difference between it and the clothing of the children of the independent labourer. It is important to add that I was taken to visit every pauper child boarded-out in these villages, so that there could be no selection of cases.

. . . .

My next visits were made at a village called Ells-rickle, high among the hills, in the south-east corner of Lanarkshire, where I saw 24 children boarded-out in the families of crofters. In several cases the head of the family, besides cultivating his few acres of ground, has a loom, at which he works at odd hours, and the homes are the ideals of comfort and thrift. Most families have a cow, some even two, and a good garden, besides the few acres of farm. Out of school hours the children work on the farm, in the garden, and help their foster parents in all the house and other work.

I saw the village school, managed by a young schoolmistress, with boys and girls of all ages learning together. The mistress told me that she had not the least trouble in managing the boys, and found not the slightest inconvenience from the mixture of boys and girls. I never saw a finer set of children, and considering the pure air, the out-door life, and the milk without stint supplied to them, it is not to be wondered at. Most of the foster parents I saw in Scotland have been taking in children for many years, a large proportion for over 20 years. They have interesting histories to tell of foster children out in the world; many of these, who have emigrated or reside in distant places, write and send little gifts to them years and years after

they have left the home.   The foster parents generally
hear of places for the children when they are of age to
go out, and the children seem always to look on the
house of their foster parents as their home.

Having been told that the districts I had visited were
exceptionally suited for presenting the boarding-out
system in a favourable light, and that, in ordinary villages in country districts, good homes in which to
place pauper children could not be found, I went to
see some orphans boarded-out by the St. George's
Hanover Square Union, in the village of Calverton in
Buckinghamshire.

These children are boarded-out according to the
rules issued by the Local Government Board.

At the parish school I saw the children boarded-out
in Calverton, and I afterwards visited the cottages in
which they were placed.

It is two years and a half since the children arrived;
they were suffering from bad ophthalmia, but the
disease did not spread to the children with whom they
were associated, and after a time they got quite well.
They have steadily grown, and strengthened in health.
The eldest of the children, a girl of 13, was very small
of her age and delicate when she arrived; she is now
a tall, strong girl.

The children call their foster parents, mother,
uncle, and aunt, according to circumstances. They
are watched over by the rector of the parish and his
wife, who tell me they have every reason to believe
that the adoption of the children is for life, and that

there will always be a home for the children when they change their place of service, or have a holiday.

The homes were selected by the rector and his wife. One home is with an old servant of the family, a laundress, who is comfortably married, and whose children are out in the world. Another, with a childless couple, the husband in good employment on the railroad. Another, with a woman who was glad of a companion for her own child of the same age. Another, with a labourer and his wife, a particularly clean, active woman, known by the rector's wife to manage her own children capitally; and so on.

I consider this specimen of the boarding-out system as highly satisfactory in every way.

APPENDIX F.

INQUIRY INTO ALL THE GIRLS SENT TO SERVICE FROM THE 17 METROPOLITAN PAUPER SCHOOLS DURING THE YEARS 1871 AND 1872.

. . . .

The object of this inquiry has been to ascertain how far the girls sent to service from every school in the years 1871 and 1872 were well conducted, and efficiently trained.

The method adopted in making the inquiry has been—

First.—From each school was obtained a list of all the girls sent to service during the years 1871 and 1872. . . .

Secondly.—Inquiries were made of the mistresses with whom the girls were placed, concerning their character, conduct, and efficiency.

. . . .

These reports were afterwards divided into four classes: Good; Fair; Unsatisfactory; and Bad.

It was originally intended to have one table for both District and Separate Schools, but in order to test its accuracy, we made, although not for publication, a table for each school.

The number of failures from the District, as compared to the Separate schools, thus came to light. Two tables are therefore given in which the results of the inquiry appear:—

[4] DISTRICT SCHOOLS

.   .   .   .   .   .

No information, owing to—

Incorrect addresses ⎤ About
Families removed   ⎬ 74 Girls.
Letters unanswered ⎦

(Information refused in 1 case.)

Information received about 245 Girls:

	Number	Per-centage
Class 1. —	28 =	11.42
Class 2. —	64 =	26.12
Class 3. —	106 =	43.26
Class 4. —	47 =	19.02
	245 =	99.82

[12] SEPARATE SCHOOLS
No information, owing to—

Incorrect addresses ⎤ About
Families removed   ⎬ 106
Letters unanswered ⎦ Girls

Information received about 245 Girls:

	Number	Per-centage
Class 1. —	51 =	20.81
Class 2. —	81 =	33.06
Class 3. —	82 =	33.46
Class 4. —	31 =	12.65
	245 =	99.98

.   .   .   .

[Mrs. Senior gives many examples, from which we select four.]

[EXAMPLE OF] GOOD.

In school 9½ years. Separate school.

Excellent character. Honest, truthful, good-tempered, willing, industrious, and very steady; clean and tidy; particularly good needle-woman; makes all her own clothes.

[EXAMPLE OF] FAIR.

Brought up in school. Separate school.

Much improved. At first was untruthful, and pilfered; could do laundry-work and common scrubbing when she came, but hardly any housework; no cooking; could not pare a potato.

[EXAMPLE OF] UNSATISFACTORY.

Brought up in school. District school.

Girl said she had never lit a fire or cleaned a grate, but as she never spoke the truth about anything, probably she lied there. On being refused leave to go out one Sunday she howled till a mob collected.

[EXAMPLE OF] BAD.

In school 7 years. Separate school.

Untruthful, dishonest, violent, and savage; threatened to stab the nurse; knew nothing of housework. This girl used to pretend that she visited her mother, who was in the workhouse, but the mistress has reason to believe that she spent her time in going about with a boy. The girl has had five situations since she left this one, and is now in workhouse.

The following letter is from one of the friends who made inquiries as to the girls who went to service in 1871 and 1872:—

MY DEAR MRS. SENIOR,

The answers given to me by the mistresses of girls sent to service from the Metropolitan pauper schools were so uniform in character, that I think the system of training must be in great measure responsible for characteristics so general, and so strongly marked. I have made inquiries as to 47 girls.

The girls were all, without exception, well taught in reading and writing. In arithmetic, so far as I could ascertain, they were fairly competent.

All, without exception, were well taught in needlework, as regards the mere execution of stitches; and all, with one exception, were unable to arrange or to do any sort of needle-work without constant supervision.

All, without exception, were well taught in the elements of religious knowledge.

All, with one exception, were very difficult and stubborn in temper, and a large majority exceedingly violent and ungovernable at times.

All, without exception, were curiously apathetic in temperament, described to me as "not caring for anything," "taking no interest," "not enjoying," "seeming like old people," &c.

All, with one exception, were stunted in growth and physical development, even where health was perfectly good.

.   .   .   .

APPENDIX G.

GIRLS WHO LEFT SCHOOL IN 1868, AFTER NOT LESS THAN FIVE YEARS IN SCHOOL.

Table of the 51 Girls whose Histories are given in the following Appendix:—

18 Girls doing well. . . .

7 Girls dropped out of sight of whom last tidings were satisfactory. . . .

16 Girls dropped out of sight of whom last tidings were unsatisfactory. . . .

3 Girls incapacitated. . . .

2 Girls of whom there is no record since they left School. . . .

2 Girls gone to relations direct from School. . . .

1 Absconded from School.

2 Dead. . . .

———

51 Total.

·　·　·　·　·　·　·　·　·

[From the 51 examples we give two.]

(25.) E. E.

ORPHAN.

Admitted, 23d October 1862.   Age 9.
Discharged, 2d April 1868.

E. E. was in first class at school. The chaplain's first report of her, two months after she had been in place, was that she was slow at work, dirty, and thoughtless, not quite truthful, but honest and good tempered, with no bad relations. The mistress, Mrs. C., said E. E. was a very worthless girl; sullen, obstinate and untruthful. Two women visited her while she was with Mrs. C. One said she was E. E.'s mother, a very low sort of person. As the girl was an orphan, this woman could not have been her mother. The other woman was a cousin, smartly dressed, and apparently not respectable. Mrs. C. said they had reason to suspect E. E.'s honesty. Some spoons disappeared in a very unaccountable manner, and the girl's manner was so unsatisfactory that they sent for a policeman, but nothing was proved. The girl, who had a mole on her forehead, bought a fortune-telling book, which predicted great things for people so marked, and the girl seemed much occupied with this subject. After a time, as nothing could be done with E. E., Mrs. C. discharged her. Mrs. C. is under the impression that E. E. is now on the streets.

.   .   .   .

(28.) S. S.

MOTHER IN WORKHOUSE.

Admitted, 19th May 1859. Age 6.
Discharged, 31st October 1868.

S. S. has once visited the school since leaving.
Said she wanted to have a place in some business
house, and seemed to have grand notions. She went to
place to a Mrs. E. She does not appear to have been
visited by chaplain. Her first mistress says that S. S.
was strong and healthy, and might have made a good
servant, but she was very self-willed, and had a most
violent temper. They gave her warning, because in a
fit of rage she threw a pail of water over their nurse,
a very respectable servant, who had been a long time in
their family. Mrs. E. thought she might perhaps do
better in a place where no other servant was kept, and
got her a very nice situation with a friend of hers,
Mrs. B.; but her conduct was no better there, and the
B.'s gave her warning. Her first mistress, feeling a
responsibility for the girl, intended to send her back
to the school when Mrs. B. parted with her, and
arranged that the man-servant should drive her back
to school in the gig. But S. S. told the man that if he
took her there she would murder him on the way, so
Mrs. E. did not insist. Mrs. E. heard from a person
whose word she could trust that S. S. was seen about
a year ago, very early one morning, sitting on a door-
step in a most deplorable condition. Had every sign
about her of leading an unsatisfactory life.

·   ·   ·   ·   ·   ·   ·   ·   ·

APPENDIX H.

SCHEME FOR SUPERVISION OF GIRLS IN PLACE.

1. Each girl on first being placed out in service by any Union shall appear before a Lady Inspector at a central office in London; the girl's name and description shall be entered in a Register, together with a character, which shall be sent with her from the School authorities. The girl shall be taken to her place by a female agent appointed by the Lady Inspector.

2. Each girl shall be officially visited in her place of service at least once in three months, and the report of how she is doing entered at the central office.

3. A post-card with address of an official at the central office shall be given to both servant and mistress, with the request that in case of the girl leaving the place, it may be sent at once to the office.

4. A plan shall be arranged by which, on one of these post-cards being received, the girl may be put in the way of a safe lodging, which shall be paid for out of her wages.

So much is already done in a different, and, as it is thought, less effective way, by all the Unions which hold themselves in a measure responsible for a girl for two years after she goes to service, or until she attains the age of 16.

By means of the voluntary efforts of ladies it is now proposed, besides this official care, to give each girl the *option* of receiving certain additional advantages, *e.g.*, lodging at a cheap rate in a central home when out of place, occasional social gatherings or treats, a safe and cheerful place in which she may pass her occasional "days out," prizes for keeping place, and good conduct, admission on beneficial terms to a clothing fund of wages.

These advantages should be offered not to workhouse girls *as such*, but generally to orphans or friendless young servants who are willing to enroll themselves as members of a "young servants' friendly society," under the management of ladies, as herein-after to be described.

It will be among the duties of the Lady Inspector to keep the voluntary and official parts of this organisation in harmonious working, directing the whole as from one head and centre.

London might be divided for this purpose into, say, five districts, in each of which the Lady Inspector would appoint a lady resident in the district to carry out, with the help of other ladies and the official (paid) visitor, such plans for the benefit of the servant girls as might be suggested or approved by the Lady Inspector.

The central lodging-house might be established, and placed under the external management of some lady who would undertake to provide the necessary funds (exclusive of the official salaries) by voluntary contributions; and the Lady Inspector (as representing the public interests) would have the ultimate voice in the rules and general regulations, engage and dismiss the matron, &c., but on the other hand not take upon herself the immediate charge of the inmates, which would devolve on the matron under the voluntary lady.

The staff of officials, to be under the immediate control of the Lady Inspector, would consist of a certain number of female visiting agents; a matron for the home or lodging-house, and a book-keeper, who would also conduct the Servants' Registry, and live at the Home (which would also be used as the central office), and of whom all inquiries would in the first place be made.

The salaries of these officials the only expense to the State.

INDEX

CPSIA information can be obtained
at www.ICGtesting.com
Printed in the USA
BVHW052355080223
658190BV00009B/236